W9-CHQ-977

Praise for
Reflections of a Grunt Marine

"An inspiring story of a 'Grunt Marine'—a participant and innovator in some of the most pivotal chapters in Twentieth Century military history." — **W.E.B. Griffin**
#1 *Wall Street Journal* and *New York Times* best-selling author of
The Corps, Honor Bound, and *Men at War* series

• • •

"*Reflections of a Grunt Marine* is a 'last hurrah' celebration of a long, remarkable, can-do panorama life by an exemplary member of the Greatest Generation. Bruce Meyers has lived a life of courage, determination, and accomplishment through three wars and much more – surviving to share his story now." — **Dave Olson**
Author of *Bonded by Water,* CIA officer during Korean War

• • •

"This book is a must read for all Marines. In reading about his part in the origins of Force Recon, one will conclude that Bruce Meyers has the fortitude and ingenuity of Ernest Shackleton, the athleticism of Jim Thorpe, and the heart and soul of a Marine. His multitude of 'was there, did that' anecdotes are fascinating, and will convince the reader he was the godfather of the 'field expedient,' a factor of great pride to all Marines who find ways to get things done. Bruce Meyers did a lot and did all well." — **Bob Rinehart**
Marine Infantry officer 1962-65 and career CIA Field Operations Officer 1966-95

• • •

"As a fellow grunt Marine, reading this motivating memoir by a true 'Marine's Marine' was most interesting and heartening. Besides being a distinguished fighting force, as seen in this book, the Marines do more. Colonel Meyers was a leader in the important work of developing and testing methods for clandestine insertion and recovery of reconnaissance teams in enemy territory. Many of those methods are used today by special force groups such as the SEALS. This was just one of the interesting parts for me in an excellent book written by a true leader of men." — **Ron Clyborne, Entrepreneur**
Served as an enlisted Marine in the early days of the Vietnam War

• • •

"*Grunt Marine* is the compelling story of a true warrior, innovator and patriot. Bruce Meyers not only chronicles a storied Marine Corps career through three wars, but reveals his critical role in honing the sharp point of the spear: Force Recon." — **John W. Hough**
former Marine Corps attorney and guard officer, 1971-1974

Publisher's Letter

When the book was first brought to my attention, I was taken by both the author and the manuscript. Bruce Meyers tells fascinating stories both in writing and conversation, with a bonus that I have been able to verify many through research. He is a "man's man," fun to visit with, but with a gentler side as well. Living alone now he credits Amy, his Corgi dog, with keeping him well through the need to walk her five times a day.

I've had the privilege of serving alongside Marines in situations abroad, both in stressful situations and during their calmer duty when guarding U.S. Embassies. My great admiration for them is certainly found in Bruce, who epitomizes the breed. Having the spirit, he also has had more varied experiences than any other I've known. Whether mountain climbing as a youngster, taking a rifle company into combat in Korea, or commanding a Marine regiment in battle in Vietnam, he's proven his mettle again and again.

In his peacetime, he was no "desk jockey," leading development of inserting and extracting reconnaissance teams through airdrops and submarines. He was the first to try out the new techniques, no matter how risky.

I hope readers will find in this book a sense of this remarkable man and his accomplishments. It's been a pleasure for me to bring them into print.

Vaughn Sherman, Publisher
Patos Island Press LLC
Edmonds, Washington
June 2015

Reflections of a Grunt Marine

by

Col. Bruce F. Meyers,

U.S. Marine Corps, Ret.

To My Fellow Colonel John Okerman USMC Thank you for your distinguished service to our Corps and Country!

Bruce F. Meyers — Colonel of Marines

Published by

Patos Island Press
Edmonds, Washington

Published by Patos Island Press
705 Spruce Street
Edmonds, Washington 98020
www.patosislandpress.com

Library of Congress Control Number
2015940876

Hardcover edition
ISBN: 978-0-9847225-9-4

Trade Paperback
ISBN: 978-0-9847225-8-7

Printed in the United States of America

Book and cover design
Jeanie James, www.Shorebird-Creative.com

Table of Contents

Col. Bruce Meyers (left) and his brother, Lt. Col. George Meyers, on Marine Corps operation south of Cua Viet River, Vietnam. March 1968.
Bruce was landing force commander, Seventh Fleet;
George commanded the Third Marine Division Amphibious Tractor Battalion.

Introduction

MY NAME IS COLONEL BRUCE F. MEYERS, USMC, retired. Upon retirement after twenty-eight years with the United States Marine Corps, I again retired, this time from the practice of law. Following the death of my wife Jo Meyers after sixty-four years of marriage, I decided to look back on my reconnaissance (recon) writings. Mind you, I turned eighty-nine years of age in August 2014.

I wrote my first book on recon in the year 2000 as *Fortune Favors the Brave (FFB)*, and initially published (five thousand copies) by the Naval Institute Press (Annapolis, Maryland). It was published by St. Martin's Paperbacks (New York) with 150,000 copies. All editions are presently sold out. After a complete review, and on advice of others more learned than myself, I determined that *FFB* was still considered a classical history of recon within the Corps. The doctrines, tactics, and equipment are still considered current, and collective opinion held that *FFB* did not need an updated rewrite version. I decided on my own to expand on areas that were not included when the decision was made by Naval Institute Press (NIP) to go with *FFB* as a current history of recon. I wrote *FFB* during the era of my twenties to forties. During that time, a significant number of assignments and commands had provided me with far greater experience than when I first published. I decided to write a new book that tapped into some of these experiences (combat and some diplomatic) that my two surviving sons, Craig and Bruce Jr. ("Boots"), had really not been privy to. I was given the benefit of three more senior ranks (major, lieutenant colonel, and colonel) and the exposure to different types of combat (Vietnam) and terrains (triple canopy jungle) and other nation's armed services, the Gurkhas (famous British fighting troops from Nepal), British troops, and the French Foreign Legion. In this review, I have tried to insert some ideas as a result of this later exposure in my life.

My commands along the way included these: the landing force of the Sixth Fleet in the Mediterranean, and the landing force of the Seventh Fleet making over-the-beach helicopter landings in combat in the Tonkin Gulf in Vietnam.

Surely my experiences commanding Khe Sanh and the Twenty-sixth Marines had great impact on me. My exposure to high levels of our government working as an aide for President John F. Kennedy at the White House and later work with the House of Representatives and Senate and as a deputy in the Office of the Secretary of Defense (OSD) added their weight as well.

I have again used most of the photographs from *FFB* (the majority by Navy and Marine Corps photographers), which add to the recounting of a more accurate story. This looking-back approach is only so that I may impart to my sons many of the reasons that I was not there for a graduation, ball game, or other significant life events when a boy is growing up.

This is a book of memories, first of scouting adventures, later of getting first real jobs, and of the mountain climbing, skiing, and swimming that many young people of our Northwest participated in at the time. I grew to believe that we become a product of this environment: our friends, our hobbies and sports, and, particularly, our education—all shape us in many ways.

This is not written as a day-by-day book, but instead, I felt it would be of greater real interest to write about events and things that influenced and shaped our later lives and personalities as we grew up and worked at our careers.

At the outset, this is the story of a recon Marine, the fins, facemasks, parachutes, and prayers that we worked with and lived with on a daily basis. I spent much of my career as an experimental parachutist and submarine diver, using all of these tools and resources in a company of outstanding marines who exhibited great bravery and fortitude, jumping out of airplanes and swimming out from submerged submarines, developing new techniques and tactics for our country. My brother, George, now deceased, was also a retired Marine colonel, but he commanded amphibious tractors.

That lays the ground work for the book. More later.

Acronyms and Definitions

Air Cav: (military slang) Air cavalry.

Amtrac: Amphibious tractor, a flat-bottomed military vehicle that moves on tracks on land or water,

AO: Air observer/controller; also, air officer.

ARC: Arc Light. Type of aerial bombing carried out from Boeing B-52s.

ARVN: Army of the Republic of Vietnam forces.

BLT: Battalion landing team. Group of approximately 1,800 Marines operating together in assigned landings.

CB or Seabee: U.S. Naval Mobile Construction Battalion, similar to Marine engineer units.

CCC: Civilian Conservation Corps. Civilian youth employment program started by President Franklin Roosevelt during the Depression. Used to build and improve national parks and other governmental construction projects.

CG: Commanding Gen..

CMC: Commandant of the Marine Corps.

CNO: Chief of Naval Operations.

CO: Commanding Officer.

DMO: Diving Medical Officer, Navy physician who is highly qualified as a doctor knowledgeable in all medical diving conditions, a highly trained and a skilled diver, qualified as a Navy diver, and medical physician. All combat swimming commanders used and relied upon these specialists for all technical diagnoses of diving-related medical problems.

DoD: Department of Defense.

DMZ: Demilitarized zone. A "no man's land" located between two- armed forces delineating an agreed to boundary. Used in Korea and also in Vietnam.

DUI: Driving under the influence, drunk driving.

FAC: Forward Air Controller. A qualified Marine pilot who assists ground unit Commander with controlling air strikes.

FFB: *Fortune Favors the Brave*, by Bruce F. Meyers. Book on reconnaissance, published by Naval Institute Press (Annapolis, MD), and in paperback by St. Martin's Press (New York).

FO: Forward observer.

Force Recon (also Force Reconnaissance): Highly trained reconnaissance unit, fully capable of assault and special operations type missions. Qualified for submarine entry using buoyant ascent and parachute ops from jet and carrier aircraft.

Grunt Marine: Usually infantry personnel who spends majority of their careers with infantry units, supported by tanks, Amtracs, artillery, and Marine air support and transport.

HQMC: Marine Corps Headquarters.

KIA: Killed in action.

LZ: Landing zone.

MARSOC: United States Marine Corps Forces Special Operations Command.

Medevac: Medical evacuation.

MCS: Marine Corps Schools, at Quantico, Virginia. Encompasses majority of Marine Corps professional instruction. TBS—The Basic School, MCU—Marine Corps University (formerly Senior School).

MCTU: Marine Corps Test Unit One.

MOH: Medal of Honor.

MOS: Military occupational specialty.

NPS: National Park Service.

NROTC: Naval Reserve Officers Training Corps

NSA: National Security Agency. Coordinates intelligence with CIA, military, and foreign governments.

OIC: Officer in Charge.

OSD: Office of the Secretary of Defense.

OPS: Operations.

POW: Prisoner of War.

PTSD: Post traumatic stress disorder.

SCUBA: Self-Contained Underwater Breathing Apparatus. Sometimes known as aqua lung. Used by divers for relatively shallow missions to 120 feet.

Seabee: U.S. Naval Mobile Construction Battalion (CB).

SEALs: U.S. Navy Sea, Air, Landing Teams. These special operations forces use diverse means of entry, especially parachute, scuba, and submarines, launched insertions and high-priority missions, highly qualified with weapons and explosives.

SecDef: Secretary of Defense.

Semper Fidelis (also ***Semper Fi*** in Marine context): Marine Corps motto. Latin term meaning "Always Faithful," it also can be translated as "Always Loyal."

SPIE: Special Patrol Insertion and Extraction

TDY: Temporary duty.

Triple Canopy: Consists of three height layers of deep jungle vegetation. The jungle floor up to about 40 to 50 feet is the lowest layer. The middle layer ranges to between 60 to 70 feet. The highest layer, at the tops of the triple canopy jungle, can range up to 130 feet above the jungle floor.

UDT: Underwater Demolition Teams. Swimmers and divers used for dive type missions during World War II. Disbanded when replaced by SEALs.

USMC: United States Marine Corps.

USMCR: United State Marine Corps Reserve.

USN: United States Navy

UW: University of Washington, Seattle, Washington.

VC: Viet Cong forces.

WW I: World War I.

WW II: World War II.

XO: Executive Officer.

CHAPTER 1

Family Roots

Here's a bit about my family before I launch into growing up and my military career. Our records go back to my grandfather, who enlisted at age seventeen for the Civil War in the spring of 1862. George P. France (yes, his last given name is the middle name for my sons; my brother, George; and me). He enlisted in the 134th Pennsylvania Volunteer Regiment[1] of the Union Army at New Wilmington, Lawrence County, Pennsylvania, on August 2, 1862, when President Abraham Lincoln was asked to raise more regiments from the northern states.

Assembling in Harrisburg, Pennsylvania, the troops were taken by train to Baltimore, Maryland, but were quickly needed to defend Washington, D.C. Robert E. Lee was approaching the capital from the southwest, through the Shenandoah Valley. His union regiment first fought in a skirmish outside of Winchester, Virginia ,and then crossed the infamous Stone Bridge at Antietam. My grandfather's diary tells the story of passing "stacks of arms and legs outside of the surgical tents." A number of the younger volunteers threw up as they passed this grisly sight.

The 134th Volunteers continued south and east toward Fredericksburg, Virginia, coming down the eastern bank as they approached the city. They began crossing the Rappahannock River, their pontoons being pushed from their banks as they crossed,

---

1   The Pennsylvania Volunteers were a Civil War infantry regiment who were raised by President Lincoln to augment regular Army units during the Civil war.

at all times "under fire from snipers" on the west bank. He was ordered to attack the heights on the western edge of the city of Fredericksburg. They were given the order to "fix bayonets" and attack up the hill to "take the heights." The three bayonet charges that he was personally involved in were bloody and his Union forces lost many of their new soldiers during the battle. They did not know at the time that they were charging against Stonewall Jackson and his very experienced Army of southerners.

Jackson was using what historians called a "sunken road." I have twice walked about that battlefield, the scene of my grandfather's unsuccessful efforts, and I beg to differ with the Civil War historians. I confirmed with the experienced national battlefield park rangers that the road was merely a typical northern Virginia wagon trail. As numerous wagons from both sides traversed this typical wagon road, the constant cutting of the wagon wheels ground the earth into a fine powder. As the troops accompanying the wagons went by, the troops picked up the rocks cut loose by the wagon wheels and merely threw them to both sides of the road. As these rocks built up on the sides of the road, it created what the historians called a "sunken road," complete with stacked rocks on either side. These rocks were quickly improved by rifleman laying in the cover and defilade, protecting the Confederate infantry in Stonewall's troops from the advancing Union forces passing through the flat areas of the city of Fredericksburg.

On December 13, 1862, following the three unsuccessful bayonet charges against Stonewall Jackson's troops, the Union forces left the Battle of Fredericksburg, crossing east, across the Rappahannock River, and going into Gen. Ambrose Burnside's mud march. They remained there the rest of the winter of 1862 in the very muddy camp with terrible snow and rain. Many Union troops died from pneumonia and flu. In reading my grandfather's diary, he spoke of having ponchos made from rubber. That was the first that I had heard that the Union Army had developed more or less waterproof ponchos made from rubber.

Burnside's mud-march soldiers did not leave their winter campsite until April of 1863. They marched south and fought their last battle in the Battle of Chancellorsville, where they were once again defeated. Withdrawing, they returned to Washington, D.C., and then on to Harrisburg, Pennsylvania, for "mustering out" (discharging). My grandfather served for a total of nine months and finally mustered out in May 1863. [2]

Then nineteen, Grandfather became a carpenter and was building oil field derricks and oil pipelines in the new oil fields in western Pennsylvania, around Titusville and

---

2   As a rifle company commander in the Korean War and a landing force commander on the east coast of Vietnam, followed by Khe Sanh, I continue to be amazed that my grandfather was neither wounded nor killed in his nine months of considerably bloody combat.

Oil City. Soon he was running five small oil derricks with very small, simple refineries at the foot of each derrick. A young fellow came to town by the name of Rockefeller. My grandfather was hired on the spot by Standard Oil. Soon, Grandfather rose to be superintendent of several Standard Oil Company refineries. He later retired to Olean, New York, where my mother, Bess France, was born in December 1884.

Our grandfather was later tragically murdered by a burglar in the basement of his summer lake house in upstate New York.

My Parents

MY MOTHER SERVED DURING WORLD WAR I as an ambulance driver in France, responsible for bringing wounded from the front lines. When she returned from her duty in France, she married one of the editors of the Olean newspaper, and they sired a child, my oldest brother, Douglas Ramsey. She and her husband eventually divorced, and she started anew by going to Seattle, now working for the American Red Cross.

Mother was serving doughnuts to Army troops at Fort Lewis, when she met my father, Herbert W. Meyers, a bachelor and an infantry major. They were married in Vancouver, Canada, in 1920. He left the Army as a major and started his own law firm in Seattle with, son of the chaplain of the U.S. House of Representatives. They started their firm, Meyers and Coudon, in the Pioneer Building at the corner of Second Avenue and Union/Yesler Way in Pioneer Square in Seattle.

Coudon was a classmate of my father's from George Washington University Law School, class of 1906. My father's family was from Baltimore, Maryland; they later moved to the Washington, D.C., area. His father, my paternal grandfather, William Meyers, was a law professor at Georgetown Law School. He became the first codifier of "The Laws of District of Columbia." I have a copy of his treatise in my own law library.

CHAPTER 2

The Formative Years
1925-1938

Although we lived in greater Seattle, our actual home was in rural Bellevue, Washington, a small truck-farming community that was becoming a commuter bedroom community for downtown Seattle. The population was a mere five hundred when I was born in 1925; we grew up with a single main street, a post office, and a grocery store. We had just two gas stations and one licensed physician.

Our schools were very basic, and we were blessed with a number of teachers who challenged us. I was in the white minority in elementary school because of the relatively large Japanese-American community. A majority of my classmates and friends *(otomodachi)* were *Nisei* (second generation Japanese, born in the United States) and their parents *(Issei)*, who were born in Japan and had emigrated to the U.S. I had two older brothers, and my parents were both college graduates.

My brother, George, was nearly three years older than I, and my brother, Douglas, was three years older than George, six years older than I. My father had been a major in the Army and was transferred to Fort Lewis, outside Tacoma, Washington, during World War I. My mother had graduated from Wells College at age twenty, growing up in Olean, New York. Her father was a vice president at Standard Oil. Upon graduation from college, she sailed to France and drove an ambulance for the American Red Cross in World War I. Our family has a thank you signed by President

Woodrow Wilson for her service driving the Red Cross ambulance in France.

Floating bridges across the twenty-two-mile-long (north-to-south) Lake Washington, in Seattle, were first built in 1939. So while growing up, we drove around Lake Washington, to the north or the south, into downtown Seattle. We frequently rode the small car/passenger ferry to Leschi in East Seattle and then rode the Yesler Way cable car to Pioneer Square in downtown Seattle. My father's law firm in Pioneer Square bit the dust fairly early in the Depression. With his background as a lawyer, he then became a revenue agent for the Federal Bureau of Alcohol, Tobacco, and Firearms (BATF). He left our family in Bellevue for periods of time to carry out his work throughout the South, the Carolinas, Kentucky, and Tennessee.

The Depression yielded the loss of many local jobs. My dad and mom were examples that one took work "where you could find it." My mother had a series of jobs, cooking lunches for the school system, and working in a bulb grower's facility. After finishing high school, my older brother, Douglas, went into the Civilian Conservation Corps (CCC). During the Depression, many of our nation's youth were "bumming rides" on the railroads ("riding the rods"). My brother George and I used to get small cans of soup from our mother (small cans of Campbell's soups were about ten cents each in those days). We would take these donations to the youth "hobo" camp that was set up on the end of the trestle that ran east of town. The cans of soup would end up being dinner for these transient youths. By my recollection, I did not notice that any females were "riding the rods."

George and I got a series of jobs mowing lawns, delivering magazines like *The Saturday Evening Post* and *The Country Gentleman,* cutting and splitting wood, and delivering occasional orders for the dry-goods store. The lot on which our house stood had a number of fruit trees—apples, plums, and some cherries. My mother had a small garden, which later became a Victory Garden in World War II. We did not, at that time, have a refrigerator, taking delivery of ice every two days from an ice truck. One of my chores was to empty the ice melt pan, as it was called, from the icebox.

CHAPTER 3

Growing Up in Rural Seattle
1938-1941

Growing up on Lake Washington led to each of our friends and all of us learning to swim. It was almost an "at birth" sort of thing. My brother and I, along with our friends, joined the Boy Scouts to improve our swimming skills.

Living in a rural community, the closest scout troop was at Hunts Point, also on Lake Washington. We quickly became Red Cross-certified lifeguards. Both of us went through the Scouts until about age fifteen or sixteen. I worked on the Boy Scout staff one summer at Camp Parsons on the Olympic Peninsula. That got me interested in mountain climbing. Our summers were spent climbing in the Olympics; Mount Anderson and The Brothers were our first mountains.

Our neighborhood had occasional deer nibbling in my mother's garden. Squirrels and chipmunks became pets. Mountain beavers, with their penchant for eating roses, led to my brother and me becoming beaver trappers of sorts. We had a neighbor, Mr. McGinity, who lived a block away on the boundary of the newly established and undeveloped Meydenbauer Beach Park. He prided himself on the fine roses that he grew in his outdoor garden that was on the edge of the park. Mountain beavers clambered up the hillside and ate many of Mr. McGinity's roses. He asked George, and me if we would "... like to make some money?" Of course we did, so we went to the local dry goods store and purchased several beaver traps at about $1.50 each.

They were known as "victor traps." The traps came with a two-foot metal chain and a metal stake, so the beaver could not chew through the trap. We were paid twenty-five cents per beaver that we trapped. Mr. McGinity was pleased, and we had a modest income to spend as we pleased. We thinned out the mountain beaver population in the area next to Mr. McGinity's property. And so his problem diminished to the point where we stopped being beaver trappers.

IN ABOUT 1937 OR 1938, my brother, George, and I became friends with Mr. Stanley Donogh, who was a neighbor on the shores of Lake Washington. He was a corporate president, CEO, and regional head of Sears and Roebuck. Obviously quite affluent, he was a great yachtsman, and he was the first amputee I had ever known. As a young man he raced motorboats. One day his small racing-boat flipped, and the engine remained running. His leg was amputated by the still-spinning propeller. With a prosthesis, he was able to swim in good form. His son, Stanley, was about my age and we became good friends during this period.

Mr. Donogh occasionally needed help running his sixty-six foot yacht, the *Zimmy*. It was a cabin cruiser that could sleep six or more. It was equipped with two twin-diesel engines. George and I would work as deck hands when the Donoghs would take their friends and family as passengers up to the San Juan Islands in northern Puget Sound. Mr. Donogh quietly paid us for these duties. George began to cut their very large lawn with a power mower during the summers. Mr. Donogh was very generous in permitting George and me to use his power tools. He had drill presses and a complete range of tools for motor repair. He always taught us how to use them properly.

The Donogh docks were always quite busy. Occasionally outboard motors would be inadvertently dropped off the docks into the water, as well as cameras binoculars, and eye glasses. The depth of Lake Washington next to the Donogh docks was about eighteen to twenty feet, too deep to have any bottom time for free-diving to look for the dropped items.

At thirteen, I began to think about building a diving helmet. I had seen a submarine movie entitled *Submarine D-1* that had some salvage and rescue diving scenes. I envisioned using a large can as a helmet, a standard fifty-foot, one-inch garden hose as a source for my air, and one of my mother's old washing machine motors. I needed a small compressor, so I went to the Seattle Goodwill store to see what they might suggest. They had several small compressors that had been used on older models of touring cars such as the Packard or Pierce Arrow. It cost me five dollars and it worked fine. I used a belt drive to run my washing machine motor. I mounted it all neatly on

The Diving Helmet

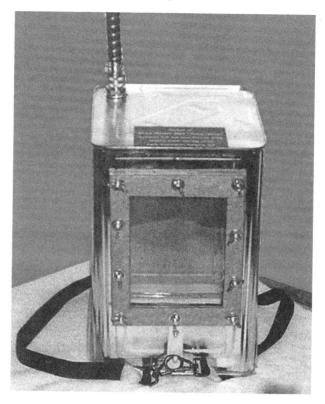

A reproduction of the operational diving helmet that the author designed when he was thirteen.

a plywood base. Mr. Donogh gave me one of his older garden hoses.

For a weight belt, I envisioned using my dad's World War I cartridge belt. I used about four building bricks hung in small cloth bags that corn meal had come in as my divers' "weight belt."

Construction of the diving helmet proper was actually pretty simple and straight-forward. I went to one of Bellevue's gas stations and asked the owner if he had any metal cans in which large amounts of oil had been shipped. He gave me a large metal container that was about eighteen inches in height and about thirteen inches on the square, top and bottom. He made sure that it was pristinely clean as I had told him what I was building. I carefully cut the bottom out of the can, leaving the reinforced ridge of about one-quarter inch all around the bottom. I then cut several pieces of plastic hose about one-quarter inch in diameter. Taking great care, I slit a line down the piece of the plastic tubing that I planned to use. I then cut smoothly rounded notches from each side of my helmet and padded the cuts on the can. The helmet would then rest on my shoulders. The tubing prevented any cuts (see photograph of my recently constructed replica, page 14). What a grand utilization of what had started its life as a simple metal five-gallon can.

The dry goods store owner had a glass cutter and he carefully cut me a piece of six-by eight-inch by quarter-inch-thick storefront glass, which was in throw-away bin, so there was no charge. Carefully, I used Mr. Donogh's drill press and saw to cut a piece of quarter- inch plywood that was to be used to attach the plate glass to the front of my diving helmet. The wooden glass retainer was about an inch-and-a-half wide that I used it to form a frame for the diver's glass faceplate on the front of the helmet.

The friendly (and now very interested) gas station owner gave me an old truck tire inner tube, from which I cut three rubber gaskets to make my diving front piece leak proof. Gasket shellac finished the job. I treated the plywood with a clear lacquer, and it too was leak proof. To hold the plywood edge surrounding my glass face plate window, I used ten wing nuts with the rounded edge facing to the outside. Every diving helmet that I observed in *Submarine D-1* used wing nuts on their face plates. Why argue with proven success?

It took me about one day to put everything together. It began to look like a real diving helmet. My last task was to hand-solder a male hose fitting on the top surface of the helmet, to which I would screw Mr. Donogh's garden hose for my air supply. Mr. Donogh reviewed the safety rules for our diving. George was going to be my diving tender. Incidentally, the entire design of my helmet, compressor, air hose, and fittings was my very own design. George did not offer any suggested changes and so, if it worked, it was all mine. We were very aware that the most dangerous aspect of using my electric washing machine motor was the use of electricity near the water. In retrospect, it would have been much safer if I had used a Briggs and Stratton type of gasoline motor, but we had to work with what we had.

I attached two pieces of quarter-inch light rope at the center of the rear of the helmet and ran them under my arms and up to the front of the helmet where I could hook or unhook them for quick release. With all the neighborhood kids watching, I slowly walked into the gently sloping water. This was the first test of actually using my self-designed helmet for salvage diving. It stayed properly low on my shoulders. As I eased deeper toward nineteen and twenty feet under water, the water slowly rose inside the helmet.

I was pleased with the working results and learned how to squat to pick things up from the bottom of Lake Washington, rather than bending forward. Water in a diving helmet always stays level, no matter what position your helmet is in, so I learned to keep my bending to a minimum and to squat retrieve items.

I had been diving for about ten minutes when George began to wonder what the impact would be by unplugging the electric cord that was powering my washing machine motor. He pulled the plug, and I could no longer hear the reassuring pump sound. The water began to rise pretty quickly, so I took a deep breath of the available air, held it, and used my quick release to dump the helmet. Instantly, it turned over and sank with no air coming through the hose. Next, I tried to dump the cartridge belt of bricks that was holding me down beneath the surface of the water. The cartridge belt was jammed and, try as I might, it would not come off.

I walked underwater toward the beach until my head was out of the water, and I could breathe again. Once on the beach, I was finally able to undo the cartridge belt. I should have made some sort of quick release but I hadn't done so. I learned from that first experience and from that point forward, the cartridge belt was rigged for quick release.

I made a beeline for George and my friends told me that it took them about a minute to get my hands from around his throat. We all were able to laugh about it later, but from then on there would be no inadvertent shutting off of my air supply under any circumstances.

I began to gain a modest local reputation as a salvage and recovery diver. Anytime anyone lost an outboard motor, or dropped a camera, eyeglasses, or binoculars into the water, they would call me, and I would dive and recover their dropped items. I did not charge for this service, but they, being grateful for the recovery of their lost things, would usually slip me a few dollars. I continued this work for another four years, until the beginning of World War II in 1942 when I entered the Navy as a midshipman-in-officer-training.

Filling Orders, Climbing Mountains, and '32 Roadster

AT FIFTEEN, I GOT A JOB at Sears and Roebuck in their mail-order warehouse to supplement the diving and deckhand revenue. At Sears I was an order-filler; my days were busy, and I was earning money towards the purchase of my first car.

For recreation, I went mountain climbing every weekend with my high school friend, Chuck Welsh, and my other climbing partners. By sixteen, I had climbed every major peak in Washington State.[1]

---

1 Mt. Rainier (climbed twice)—14,410 ft.; Mt. Adams—12,276 ft.; Mt. St. Helens (before it blew its top in 1980, Saint Helens had been 9,677 ft., but after the eruption it dropped to 7,969 ft.).; Mt. Baker—10,775 ft; Mt Olympus in the coastal Olympic Mountains—7,969 ft.; and Glacier Peak—10,451 ft..

Summer 1941. Climbing in Washington State's Cascade Mountains.

When I turned sixteen, I took some of my summer earnings and bought a used 1932 Model A roadster with a rumble seat for fifty dollars cash. On occasion, I would pay the twenty-five-cent toll for the newly constructed floating bridge across Lake Washington and drive into Seattle to Franklin High School. Looking back on that purchase, it helped me to grow up and gain more responsibility. It also gave me an awareness of the value of hard work and saving my money.

At Franklin High School, I made the honor society and became the president of the student body. I played varsity football at Franklin, and I ran the mile in track. Herb Bridge, son of a local Seattle jeweler, used to run in track with me, and we became lifelong friends. Both of us entered the Navy, the Naval Reserve Officer Training Corps (NROTC) for me and initially an enlisted tour for Herb. Following graduation and commissioning from the University of Washington, Herb had a very successful career enlarging his dad's jewelry store into a large jewelry store empire. Herb retired as a rear admiral in the Navy Reserve.

CHAPTER 4

Summer of '42

Borrowing the title for this section from the book and 1971 movie of the same name seemed appropriate when I look back some seventy-plus years to my last summer as a civilian. My memories of the "Summer of '42" are good ones. I spent that summer as a forest fire lookout in the central Cascade Mountains of Washington State, some thirty-five miles east of Seattle and about twenty miles north of North Bend, Washington.

World War II, with its fiery inception with the Japanese attack on Pearl Harbor December 7, 1941, was fresh in all of our minds. A number of defensive postures had been taken by the United States. One of them was the closing off of all civilian hiking and climbing in the Pacific coastal forest and mountain areas. The reason was to preclude any Japanese attacks from torching our forests.

At the Mile-High Forest Fire Lookout

AS A RESULT of my fairly extensive climbing and outdoors background, I was offered a summer job as a forest fire lookout in the Cascade Mountains just east of Seattle. I applied and was hired for the job by District Ranger Paul Piper, whose ranger station was in North Bend, Washington, a city in the Cascade foothills about twenty-five miles east of Seattle. I was still only sixteen years old, but I knew I would turn the required seventeen years while on the lookout. Looking back, in a way I have no regrets for lying about my age. With the war going on, many people misstated their ages for various reasons. I knew in my heart that I was far more qualified to be assigned to a remote lookout deep in the Cascade Mountains than many others.

We underwent intensive fire-fighting training and learned how to use the Osborne Firefinder to locate fires. I was assigned to be the primary lookout, and my assistant at the Bare Mountain lookout was Bob McIver, a seventeen-year-old athlete from Seattle Prep, a large prominent Catholic high school.

Ranger Piper asked me to bring Bob up to speed on his survival and outdoor skills. I did as asked, and we became a solid fire-finding and fire-fighting team. We also became good friends and worked well together at the remote Bare Mountain lookout, located above the north fork of the Snoqualmie River. The unpaved mountain road leading north to the lookout area only ran twelve miles north from the ranger station at North Bend. Thus, we had to be "packed in" by a Montana packer on six pack horses and one pack mule. We packed our three months of food onto the pack animals and entrusted Jess, our Montana packer, to get us up to the lookout.

I learned one trick, involving eggs, about packing food for the entire summer. My mother suggested that we should take about six dozen eggs. I liked oatmeal for breakfast, so she suggested opening each of the six tube-shaped packages of oatmeal and dumping it all out. She then had me put a three-inch layer of oatmeal on the bottom, carefully place about four eggs inside the package, pad the eggs with more oatmeal and then cover them with another layer of oatmeal, and so on until the circular package was filled with padded eggs and oatmeal. Not one egg broke on the trip up to our lookout. Having no refrigeration of any kind at the lookout, I used snow from several snow drifts, which remained frozen during the entire summer (remember the lookout was on a mountain top in the west center of the Cascades). The whites of the eggs began to look a bit yellow in color by the end of the summer, so we "deep-sixed" the remaining few eggs.

Packing in on the six pack horses and one pack mule was an event in itself. All of our food for the summer was packed into compact packages and secured to the Army-style horse pack frames worn by our pack mule and horses. Only one of our pack horses slipped in the ascent. Jess and I climbed down to our fallen friend. Fortunately, after we took the pack off, the horse stood up without any apparent injury. If that pack horse had broken its leg, we would have had to shoot it. We repacked him and were able to get to the lookout by about 11 a.m. the next day.

Pack horses do not like bears. Although we had no problems with bears, I attribute

Bear Mountain Lookout at 5,353 feet in the southern Cascade Mountains.
The lookout is about twenty miles north of North Bend, Washington and operated by the U.S. Forest
Service. The lookout is cabled and anchored to a knife-edge ridge. Bruce and his assistant,
Bob McIver, manned the station from June through September 1942.

that to the fact that Jess, Ranger Piper (who was dropping us off for the summer), McIver, and I must have been enough "people" to make the bears avoid us and our pack string. The animals spent the night whinnying and snorting to each other and stamping their feet. Piper reviewed all of our prior fire locating and fighting instructions and gave us a final review on use of the firefinder and off he and Jess went back down the trail.

BARE MOUNTAIN LOOKOUT was a standard twelve-foot square building, placed on the knife ridge of the summit of the mountain. There was a small, flattened-out area on the ridge, which permitted us to walk around only three sides of the lookout. The western side, facing towards Seattle, thirty-five miles to the west, was at the top of a sheer cliff with 350-feet down being our "first bounce" if we fell off. The five-foot windows on all four sides started about ten inches from the floor at the base, with the top edge ending just below the flat ceiling. This permitted 360 degrees of viewing with the Osborne Firefinder in the center. I taught McIver to "rope up" with climbing rope, so anytime we window-washed or worked on the roof we were securely roped in. It was more something to do rather than a chore. The frequent summer rains and accompanying winds did a pretty good job of ensuring that we had good, clear windows to view the surrounding mid-Cascades terrain. Anytime we had to adjust the radio antennae on the roof, we roped up. Being a remote lookout, there was no electricity, so we used Coleman lanterns. We spoke by Forest Service shortwave radio every two hours during the day to the other lookouts: Three Fingers Lookout at Bellingham, Washington; Granite Peak near Snoqualmie Pass; and Stampede Pass Lookout on an east-west alternate crossing of the Cascade Mountains, to the south of what eventually became Interstate Route 90 (I-90).

Some lookouts with two occupants, not husband and wife, which became quite common in later years, would have conflicts between the two personalities. Aware of this, McIver and I always ensured that we gave each other space, and we tried to take short trail checks to observe our resident bears. Our plan worked well, and we had no such problems.

Forest service lookout habitats are built for service, not comfort. We had one glass entry door and each of the four walls were glass, running virtually from the floor to the ceiling. Our one seating chair was mounted on four glass insulators, thus keeping us off the floor, in the event that lightning struck the lookout. Built along each of the two walls were two rope-laced eight-inch-high wooden bunks, perfect for cotton mattresses. Bob and I both slept in our own sleeping bags. There was one small table on which we kept and operated our shortwave forest service radio. I had a small battery-operated AM radio, which we listened to for war news and music.

Lightning Was Always a Danger on Lookouts

THE CASCADE MOUNTAINS are particularly known for both their individual lightning strikes as well as for the sheet lightning. Lightning has a tendency to follow down smoke particles rising from a cast all-metal cooking stove. The minute we became aware of possible lightning conditions, we would put out our fire, and undo and take down the stove pipe on the interior of the lookout, from just below the ceiling of the lookout to its entry into the rear top of our stove. We knew the propensity of lightning to strike the highest thing on the lookout peak. Thus, each of the lookout roofs was well grounded. There was a very strong one-quarter-inch square copper wire grounding that was attached to the lookout roof. It ran from a central lightning rod down each of the four sides of the pyramid-shaped roofs that came together to make our lookouts appear as a peaked roof.

Our closest neighbor was an old gold miner who worked a small gold mine along a creek that formed the drainage for the north fork of the Snoqualmie River. He knew where we were, some two thousand feet above him at the lookout. We never saw him during the entire summer.

Seattle was the home of, and the main place of manufacture, of the famous B-17 "Flying Fortresses" of World War II. Each one of the 6,981 newly manufactured bombers made in Seattle had to be flown for two hours of flight time in order to work out all the bugs or discrepancies before turning them over to Army Air Corps pilots. The test flights of the newly minted bombers would fly around the skies surrounding Seattle and the Boeing field. Many would fly twenty to thirty miles eastward and fly over the very scenic but very rugged Cascade Mountains. McIver and I would see these aircraft flying over our mountain. We would take a small signal mirror (similar to those issued and carried by all military pilots to use for survival) and flash the pilots ,and, out of interest or boredom, they would roll over and make a diving run on our lookout. The roar of the engines would be tremendous and nearly earth shattering. The rush of wind from their dive would nearly tear our flag off its flagpole. The pilots would pull out right above us from their dive and they would waggle their wings (a greeting done by pilots all over the world as an acknowledgment of our flashing our signal mirror and their saying "hi") and give us a thumbs-up.

With the exception of small mountain field mice, most of the wild animals kept their distance from us. Whistling marmots, with a piercing whistle, would take up a perch on the edge of any abyss and, watching us very carefully, whistle to each other or to us. We became used to them and we would give them names that bespoke of their personalities. Coyotes would howl most evenings, talking to each other back and forth across intervening valleys and crags.

The entire north side of Bare Mountain ridge was covered with wild blueberries. Bob and I craved those wild blueberries. We would only have to go about fifty yards down our trail to get them. We would fill our plastic bags with the lush berries, going around the blind side of a large blueberry bush. Around the other side would come a brown bear doing the same thing, picking and eating as he or she went. There were no grizzly or black bears in our area. Once either the bear or we spotted the other, we would immediately slowly turn and move in the other direction, avoiding any sort of confrontation. We got used to each other's habits and it worked out well, sharing the remote mountain with the bears.

A lookout's day can be long and, if one lets it, lonely. We did everything we could do to avoid such feelings. Every two hours, one of us would have to check in by radio. All similarly manned lookouts did the same. Any other station could break in to our network, so there was never a problem about being on the radio. One good byproduct of our contact with other lookouts was the exchange of cooking recipes. My mother wisely sent me off with a fairly simple cookbook. She ensured that I had the Betty Crocker recipes for cookies, bread, and crusts for our blueberry dishes. We had blueberry pancakes, blueberry cookies, and fresh blueberries in our cereal. Our supply of oatmeal, six large tube cartons, lasted all summer. My recipe for a bowl of blueberries: Add some water and sugar, and bring all to a boil and then make a biscuit dough top. When browned it became crusty and topped off what we called blueberry cobbler or just plain blueberry pie. These all turned out to be very tasty. We became pretty good cooks by summer's end.

Since we were a remote lookout, our lightning strikes would be too far in the forest for a fire crew to come in and take care of them. Once the determination of too far in was made, Ranger Piper would give Bob and me turns during which one of us would go to the lightning strike location.

Frequently, lightning would pick a single, tall, dead snag tree to light a potential forest fire. Our fire-fighting gear consisted of a head cover, similar to those "bush hats" worn in Vietnam; a pair of gloves; a pack with a forty-gallon hand pump, and a Pulaski tool. The Pulaski was a forest service invention. It consisted of an ax head on one side and a ground hoe (for digging fire lines in rocky soil) on the other side. If we could reach the top of the snag with our hand-pump, we would try to hit the top of the burning/smoking snag. We would fill the five-gallon metal water container, mounted on a backpack, with stream water or ice melt or snow from the many of the mini- glacier tarns (small mountain lakes" that populate that area of the Cascade Mountains). We would use the hoe side of the Pulaski to run a fire line in a circle around the snag. If we could, we would then use the ax side of the Pulaski to cut the snag down. We had to be careful when the snag hit the ground, it could not roll down the side of the mountain to start another fire further down the mountain. It worked and we never had to call in a fire crew for help. For most of the lightning strikes, the hand-administered pumping action of the hand pump would shoot a stream of water about forty feet. When it was above that height, we either had to drop the snag or radio for some help from a fire crew.

When Ranger Piper came up to relieve us and to secure the lookout by shuttering and locking it up, he came with Jess the Montana packer about the first week of September 1942. We brought out all spare communications radio batteries for the trip out. Bob and I had been in the bush, on the lookout, for three months. We had not been around any vehicles that entire time. We found ourselves getting a bit jumpy for the first hour or so back in the real world. That summer of '42 was the last time that lookout was used. In following years the lookout mission was done in remote areas by aircraft observers. It was a great summer, and both of us gained a great deal from our experience.

We each had enough high school credits to graduate in December 1942, so we did and immediately entered the military.

CHAPTER 5

Naval Officer Training
1943-1945

Following a rather informal graduation from Franklin High School in the principal's office, I immediately applied for entry as a midshipman in the University of Washington's Naval Reserve Officer Training Corps (NROTC). At age seventeen, I was immediately sworn in but not put on active duty until later that summer. Initially, we were enrolled as regular university students with an average course load of fifteen credits per quarter, and an additional equivalent of three hours per week of classes in Naval science and tactics. Thus, our actual university course load was about eighteen hours per week.

We received excellent hands-on instruction in seamanship, shipboard procedures, some gunnery and small arms weapon training, and sending and receiving Morse code. All of this practical instruction was given by our two master chief petty officers, "Salty" Sincere and Harmony. I had to do a bit of doubling up so that I could catch up to my classmates who had been taking these same courses for the past five months.

In January 1943, I began to pay my own tuition, which continued for six months until we were called to active duty on July 1, 1943. I worked every weekend as a permit longshoreman in Local 1-19 of the International Brotherhood of Longshoreman located on the waterfront in Seattle. I would peg my small wooden peg into the union hall wall board opposite my name and permit number, to indicate that I wanted to work. Usually my brother, George, and I would peg in together and, generally, we would be assigned the same gang on one of the numbered docks (e.g., "Pier 38") on the Seattle waterfront. Our pay was much higher than minimum wage. Many longshoreman who worked full-time as longshoreman during the week would opt not to peg in on the weekends.

Both George and I played football for the (UW) Huskies. Thus, the spring training as UW football players worked with George and me as "permit men" on assigned gangs. We quickly learned many technical safety aspects of being a longshoreman, such as carrying a longshoreman's hook for lifting off hatch covers from "the square of the hatch." By working on both Saturday and Sunday, we could make close to a hundred dollars each over the weekend. That helped a great deal in paying our college costs. We had moved away from our parent's house in Bellevue and were living in a fraternity house at the university. This pretty much ended living with our parents, but we would visit them whenever we could, often on the weekends when we did not longshore.

WORLD WAR II made us all grow up more quickly beyond our teenage years. While serving as a midshipman, I was assigned temporary sea duty from December 1942 to February 1945, in between semesters or quarters (terminology changed during the time that we were there). Our Naval Academy skipper Capt. Eric Barr[1], was apparently trying to replicate his aggressive Naval Academy experience by combining a heavy academic rigor with as much practical experience for his midshipman as possible. This was to better prepare us for fleet duty that we each faced during World War II. We thought he was pretty salty in his own right and we all respected his counsel and advice. We were assigned to various types of naval vessels for these periods between semesters.

Many of our classmates did not participate in these voluntary NROTC "cruises." I took advantage of every opportunity that I could to gain practical shipboard experience. Of the more than one hundred in the class of '45, only twenty-five or so classmates participated in these voluntary at-sea experiences. I had made my personal decision when I entered the NROTC to become a Marine officer. I was influenced somewhat by George who, about the same time, had enlisted in the Marine V-12 officer training program at UW. But I was influenced even more by a family friend, retired Marine Maj. Frank Armstead, a "China Marine[2]," who regaled us with sea stories and tales of his duty in South and Central America and World War I. We

---

1   Capt. Barr had earned the Navy Cross from submarine duty in World War I in the old "S"-boats.
2   China Marine: one who had duty in China during the 1920s and 1930s.

NROTC Midshipman Bruce Meyers (1943, age 17).

listened to these stories with avid interest.

IN RETROSPECT, I enjoyed each of my three cruises and learned a lot about shipboard life and duties. My first cruise was aboard an escort carrier. I was assigned to the USS *Casablanca* (CVE-55). To fulfill the desperate need for small aircraft carriers to escort our convoys taking our troops overseas to the battlefields of Europe and to the Orient, Kaiser shipyards and others began to mass-produce Jeep carriers, completing nearly one each week. The *Casablanca* was 512 feet from bow to stern with a sixty-five foot, three-inch beam. She had a light hull and the following armament: one five-inch dual-purpose gun, twenty 20mm Oerlikin cannons, and sixteen Bofors 40mm antiaircraft guns. She had a complement of about three hundred and could handle about twenty-eight aircraft, usually Grumman F-4 or F-6 fighters, with a mix of bombers such as the Douglas AD or torpedo bombers such as the TBF or TBM. *Casablanca* had a complete training crew that made each crewman an instructor. Thus, when new assignees would come aboard, the crewman instructor would teach each individual seaman their job, twenty-four hours a day, seven days a week for two weeks. This is how the Navy was able to get new sailors trained to man a new escort carrier every other week. It was an amazing program and turned out a hundred new crews to man the one hundred-plus escort carriers that Kaiser was building.

This experience served me well when I later served at sea as a senior officer in commanding Special Landing Force Alpha of the Seventh Fleet on the helicopter carrier LPH *Iwo Jima* during my early duty in the Vietnam War. I had also commanded the landing force of the Sixth Fleet in the Mediterranean (Med) as a lieutenant colonel doing seven months of deployed duty as the 911 force of the Med. I had just completed my year of navigation instruction at the end of my second year as a midshipman when Capt. Barr, professor of naval science and tactics, offered me duty as an assistant navigator aboard an APA bound from Seattle's Pier 91. In mid-1944 we traveled south to San Pedro, California, with a stop in San Francisco. The APA was the USS *Sandoval* (APA-193), a 455-foot troop transport with a sixty-two foot beam. The assigned navigator had been commissioned for about three years and was most helpful. He let me do all of the daily star sightings and experiencing a real course on the sextant. I shall never forget my entry into San Francisco bay in a very thick, deep, right-down-on-the-water fog. On the bridge I was monitoring our type "S" radar, which was pretty primitive for such navigation at the time. I kept our speed at about five knots ("dead slow"), and our type "S" (as I remember) was keeping us right in the center of the main channel going underneath the Golden Gate Bridge. I could see other vessels (mostly Navy vessels) coming out of San Francisco bay. Coming into the bay, we bore to the right, which gave us appropriate clearance of each other. I suggested to my navigator/instructor that I would feel more comfortable if he would permit me to "double up" on the lookouts on both wings of the bridge, and also on our bow. He concurred, so I quickly had six sets of eyes besides mine and the navigator's watching forward. We still could not see the brightly painted yellow undergirders on the Golden Gate Bridge. Just as we started, under where the bridge was supposed to be the fog magically lifted, cleared, and blew away. I shouted a hearty "thank God" to commemorate my successful navigation from Seattle's Pier 91 to San Francisco. Standing behind me, the ship's regular navigator said, "Nice job, midshipman, well done." I sighed with relief at that point, and our hearts all returned to normal. It was the nicest compliment that I received while serving as a midshipman. I learned much from that two-week cruise and became a better officer of the naval services because of this duty.

For my last midshipman sea duty, I was assigned to a patrol craft (PC), with a narrow twenty-three-foot beam. The British Navy refers to this type of vessel as a *corvette*. She was quite small for extended sea duty. We were assigned to patrol duty off the west coast of Vancouver Island and the mouth of the Straits of Juan de Fuca on the Northwest Washington coast searching for Japanese submarines. I served as a junior officer of the deck (JOOD) and stood four-hour watches on the bridge of the USS *Hellhammer*. She was lightly armored. We were equipped with sonar for the location of enemy submarines. We had a small deck gun (a three-inch fifty caliber, as I remember) on the foredeck. Once a submarine was located, our mission was to drop depth charges from the two racks of depth charges mounted on our fantail or fire small depth charges from the K-gun on our foredeck. The coastal weather was miserable, and I endured this duty, and learned a lot, but I did not care for it.

Duty on the *Hellhammer* made me appreciate all of my future duties on the five submarines that I served on while serving as a force recon Marine: USS *Perch*, USS *Sealion*, USS *Queenfish*, USS *Bream*, and USS *Ronqil*.[3] It was always a pleasure to submerge when there was "mucky weather" and slip beneath the rough seas that would occasionally cause problems on the surface.

Firefighting

SHORTLY BEFORE WE WERE COMMISSIONED, we underwent shipboard firefighting school. This proved to be an excellent and practical hands-on school that stood each of us in good stead for wherever we served.

• • •

In later commands at sea and on the ground, we had aircraft crash into our areas. We knew what to do to rescue injured crews and to limit fire damage as best we could. As a lieutenant colonel serving on a brigade staff in Camp Pickett, Virginia, in my duty with the Second Marine Division during 1964, a pilot suffered night vertigo and literally flew his helicopter into our command post on the ground. We were able to get the pilots, crew, and passengers from the burning wreckage, but despite my best efforts, one of my Marines was trapped beneath the burning wreckage and I was unable to extricate him before the aircraft was completely engulfed in aircraft-fuel-fed flames. Although we were later officially recognized for our efforts, we all felt helpless at the loss of our Marine who was crushed and burned in the crash. The Navy-Marine Corps Medal, the highest Navy and Marine corps medal for noncombat, was awarded to each of the four of us who did our best. I was burned a bit on my feet, face, and arms when I drove a burning radio jeep from the scene, but I healed quickly so there were no post-burn problems.

At Khe Sanh, we had numerous aircraft that were either shot down or lost power and crashed. Col. David Lownds, whom I relieved as regimental commander of the Twenty-Sixth Marines at Khe Sanh in April 1968, lost a Lockheed C-130 Hercules shortly before our change of command. Former Marine combat correspondent from WW II, David Douglas Duncan, now an author and a civilian combat correspondent, had his camera and got some great photos of Lownds' C-130 burning on the runway.

3   At that time submarines were named after fish.

Author and three men under his command receive Navy-Marine Corps Medal for efforts to rescue a flyer from burning wreckage.

I lost a C-130 inbound to off-load replacements and high-priority gear. The aircraft had touched down, and on its run out, while slowing down to exit the runway, it was rocketed and attacked by North Vietnamese rocket fire from just across the Laotian border near Lang Vei. Its fuel cells, which were in the wings just above the engines, were pierced by the Vietnamese rockets. This sprayed JP4 high octane aviation fuel onto the red-hot engines. The entire left wing was burning. The pilot exercised a high degree of proficiency in steering the still slowing Hercules off the only active runway to finish its burn. Had he not done this brilliant pilotage, it would have burned on the runway, which would have fouled our only runway and left us even more vulnerable.

Our firefighting gear at Khe Sanh was extremely limited, and I watched one of my Marines attempt to use a large, hand-operated fire extinguisher with flame retarding foam. He made valiant, but ineffective, efforts to put out the fire on the burning transport. Despite the intensity of flames engulfing the aircraft, our Marines entered the aircraft and were able to get out all passengers and crew. The only person killed in this crash was Felix Poilan, a French planter who had established Khe Sanh as a tobacco plantation, which grew native crops of tobacco.

Early on when the siege had started, the Third Marine Division ordered evacuation of Felix Poilan and his wife to Dong Ha some hundred miles to the south to sit out the siege. We felt devastated having to notify Felix's widow of her husband being killed in the crash. We had felt on the day of his crash that the siege was coming to an end and it would be safe to come back. How wrong we were. I nominated the brave pilot, who did such a superb job in steering off the runway, for an award of the Distinguished Flying Cross.

CHAPTER 6

Commissioned Marine Officer
1945

M y three fellow Marine Corps selectees and I, from a class of one hundred midshipman, were now commissioned as Marine lieutenants in February1945. The four of us went cross-country by train, taking almost five days, to Quantico, Virginia, to the Marine Corps schools. Quantico is about thirty miles due south of Washington, D.C., on the Potomac River, just north of Fredericksburg, Virginia. We spent a busy five months learning to be infantry platoon leaders. This infantry school was called the Platoon Leaders Class (PLC). Here we fired virtually every weapon that the Marines used during World War II: the M-1 Garand infantry rifle, the M-1 Carbine, the Browning automatic rifle (BAR), Thompson submachine guns, the light machine guns, shotguns, both 60mm and 81mm mortars, flame throwers, and explosives of all sizes and kinds. We threw hand grenades and fired antitank bazookas; we rode and landed across the Potomac River from amphibious tractors (Amtracs); and we rode on tanks, trucks, and many jeeps. We learned to call in artillery fire and direct air strikes on ground targets.

Every day was filled with practical, hands-on infantry experience. We learned to field strip and assemble every weapon or piece of equipment that we were trained on. In comparison to what our enlisted Marines were learning in boot camp (at either Parris Island, South Carolina, or San Diego, California), our PLC ended up being about three boot camps, end-to-end. When we graduated, each of us felt far more prepared as second lieutenants, ready for further training or to be assigned as platoon leaders in a combat unit.

We worked hard and, from liberty call at noon on Saturdays to evening check-in on Sundays, we took the Richmond, Fredericksburg and Potomac train (RF&P) to Washington, D.C., and many partook of adult beverages and tried to pick up the myriad of young women who flocked to an expanded Washington, D.C. because of the war effort.

Instead of taking the train, sometimes four or five of us would take a cab from Quantico to Washington, D.C. We split the cost of the cab, and we were much cleaner upon arrival in D.C. Wartime trains were notoriously dirty and smoke-filled from going through a half-dozen railroad tunnels between Quantico and Washington, D.C.

After participating about four such weekends of intensive dating and partying, I backed down a bit. I had noted a small airport that we drove by twice a weekend. I noted a sign that read "Learn to Fly $10 per hour." I was making a hundred and fifty dollars a month as a lieutenant. I figured that I could spend a bit of that doing what I had longed to do for many years, learning to fly. Five weekends later, I had soloed after eight hours of flight training, and with care and good judgment I could fly myself anywhere. That started me on a sixty-three-year hobby of flying mostly fixed wing and land planes. Over the years, I have owned two aircraft, and, after retiring from the Marine Corps, I spent nine years building my own plane. I was able to rent planes wherever I was transferred while in the service. Initially, I flew in Virginia, and then later in California, Washington, Japan, Great Britain, Australia, and New Zealand.

CHAPTER 7

From Quantico to the End of World War II
1945

After Quantico, in July of 1945, many of us who had completed PLC were given assignments requiring more or specialized training before assignment into combat units. George chose to train as an amphibious tractor (Amtrac) officer. Prior to assignment from Quantico, students were each given a series of tests to identify specialized talents, training, or background that would provide us with assignments or include us in a particular military occupational specialty (MOS).

George and I scored high in mechanical aptitude—we were only one point apart in our Minnesota Mechanical Aptitude (MMA) scores. I have to conjecture that we tested high because both of us had purchased Ford Model A cars as teenagers. We had worked on them, tuned the engines, and done our own modest repairs. Plus, we had been trained to use tools when we worked for Stanley Donogh. I had also built my own diving helmet. I was told that my mechanical aptitude score qualified me to train as a tank officer. We were advised that the Marine divisions were short of qualified tank officers. They asked me if I would train in tanks. I was not too eager to get into tanks, but the assignments officer was persuasive, so I agreed to train at Camp Pendleton's Officers' Tank School. Tank school and Amtrac school were next to each other at Pendleton, so we both ended up completing our respective schools close to each other. This turned out to be right at the end of World War II.

The atomic bombs had been dropped and most overseas troops began to return to the States. Although the Marine Corps was going to be cut back massively, George and I, newly commissioned, were going to have to remain on active duty for some time. We were assigned to units at Camp Pendleton. Immediately after the end of the war, there was a great emphasis within the armed services to welcome back the returning veterans (from the Pacific for ninety-five percent of returning Marines) so there arose a good-sized program of interservice sports. George stayed in Amtracs at the Boat Basin, the harbor for Camp Pendleton, and both of us played the season with service football for the Camp Pendleton team.

Our Last Active Duty of World War II

I WAS ASKED if I had done any swimming before entering the Marines. I told the officer screener that I had qualified as a lifeguard and that I had done some helmet diving and built my own diving helmet. With that background, they reassigned me to a staging regiment which was commanded by Col. Herman Hannekan.[1] The staging regiment was tasked to provide sea, surf, and land survival training to all Marines headed for the Pacific Theater. Much of this survival training was also used in training personnel being sent to China for occupation duties.

Replacements required training in swimming and certain combat skills. I was assigned as a combat swimming officer and instructor. Among the subjects that I was asked to teach were knife and club fighting and hand-to-hand combat. I had a special class for all Marine aviators going overseas for surf and sand survival. Santa Monica former chief lifeguard Lug Carlusi (then a Marine sergeant) was an outstanding instructor and taught with a knowledgeable, hands-on approach. He was respected by each of his students. Knowing how to save one's own life became a great motivator for each of the Marine pilots who were our students. My combat swimming platoon had become a haven for recon Marines returning from duty with the Fifth Amphibious Reconnaissance Battalion under the legendary leadership of Maj. Jim Jones, father of one of our later USMC commandants.

---

1   For his duty in Haiti as a sergeant in 1919, Col. Hannekan had been awarded the Medal of Honor.

CHAPTER 8

Flying
1945-2010

A s I began to write this book, I became aware of how much my hobby of flying privately in general aviation airplanes, such as my Piper Cub and Aeronca Champ and the Cessna 120s, 140s, and 172s that I used to rent, all made an imprint on my life. I learned to fly helicopters in Vietnam mainly for my own survival. After retirement, while practicing law and later as a law school associate dean, I flew my own J-3 Cub airplane from Seattle to the Arctic Circle, a great adventure. I also learned to fly seaplanes, allowing me take my family to more distant lakes and rivers. I ended up with almost one thousand flight hours as pilot-in-command.

While serving in Vietnam during my command of the Twenty-Sixth Marines, after Khe Sanh and transfer from the Third Marine Division south to the First Marine Division, I would be assigned a helicopter for transit from one unit to another. Most of these would be Huey utility helicopters. Frequently we would fly into "hot zones" (landing zones taking heavy fire). One always likes to be as safe as possible, even though I was involved in a dangerous profession as a colonel commanding a Marine infantry regiment. I knew that most utility helicopter pilots, aware that they were frequenting dangerous landing zones, would unofficially teach their crew chiefs to fly in the event that they (the pilots) were shot and wounded. Then the crew chief could take the controls or at least help the wounded pilot getting the airplane back to their base.

By 1968, I had logged some eight hundred hours as a pilot in command, always of fixed-wing, general aviation aircraft. When I would get my usual daily chopper, it would be equipped with one pilot (usually a young captain or first lieutenant) and two sets of controls. Unofficially, I reasoned that if I could get several of our Marine aviators to "check me out" or train me to fly, in the event of our primary pilot being wounded or incapacitated, it would add some additional safety on that aircraft. With my fixed-wing pilot time, I felt that they could check me out in pretty short order.

All of the pilots seemed impressed, apparently, with the fact that this grunt colonel wanted to be checked out as a safety precaution. They started by "following me through" on our flights on the controls. I would take the helicopter from a two-foot hover to flying the mission to returning to the selected landing zone (LZ) in a hover. At that point, the Marine pilot would land the last two feet. Thus, technically, I did not takeoff or land, that was always done by an appropriately qualified Marine aviator. At least that is what we were going to tell the board (accident investigations board), if there was an incident involving my flying.

I had adapted pretty quickly, and, by the third week of the assigned pilot following me on the controls, I had been taking the bird from the two-foot hover, flying the mission, and returning to the two-foot hover. One of the young captain aviators nearly blew my cover. He mentioned to one of the crew chiefs that "the old man was not a bad chopper pilot." The crew chief was initially stunned to discover that this non-Marine-aviator (me) had been doing ninety-five percent of the past three weeks of flying, but he was OK with that. The crew chief, and now my staff, Lt. Col. Roger Hagerty and Maj. Buck Lumpkin, S-4, now were aware that I was doing most of the recent flying. My regiment finished our deployment on the task requiring so much daily helicopter flying, and we were transferred to another regimental mission. There was never any official mention of my chopper flying and that ended any problem of officials ever learning about it and having to possibly discipline the pilots or me. At that point, in retrospect, my twenty-three years of general aviation flying had paid off. I wanted to do everything I could to return to my wife and our three sons back in Seattle. For the record, I never logged an hour of my twenty to twenty-five hours of Vietnamese chopper time.

Three "Deadstick" Aircraft Landings in Sixty-Five Years of Flying

THERE IS A SAYING AMONG OLDER PILOTS that "any aircraft landing that you can walk away from is a good landing." I learned to fly when I was a nineteen-year-old Marine lieutenant, just finishing Platoon Leaders Class (PLC) at Quantico,

Virginia. It was July 1945. I had just gotten my student pilot's license and had orders to go to Camp Pendleton for a tank officer's class. I turned twenty that summer and began building my flight hours to get the necessary thirty to thirty-five hours to be eligible to get my private license. I learned more about flying over the next sixty-four years than I ever could have imagined. Each time that I had to land deadstick—no operating aircraft engine turning a propeller at sufficient RPMs to keep the aircraft flying and in the air—I learned a little bit more about flying.

• • •

In 2005, just before I ceased active flying, the Federal Aviation Association (FAA) honored me for fifty-five years of flying with a nice certificate designating me as a master pilot. That meant that I had not pranged an aircraft in more than fifty years of flying. I did land three times without an engine. Since I am here writing about my memories, let me share these experiences with you. My sources are from my five black-colored aircraft log books that I used to keep track of my flights, where I went, what the flight and aircraft conditions were, and, for those logs with instructors' names, their name and pilot's license number, and aircraft conditions.

DEADSTICK LANDING ONE.

Piper J-5 Cub Landing Off Airport: The first incident occurred in Oceanside, California, at a small private airstrip just north and east of Oceanside. I was still learning to fly. I had hired a great instructor, Al Griffith, and he was helping teach me all of the nuances and flight maneuvers to get me through the FAA oral, written, and flight exams to qualify me for my private license. On May 5, 1946, I took my final flight check with Al in preparation for the FAA flight check to be held on May 12, 1946.

Continuing to fly that day after satisfying my instructor, I was just taking off solo from Oceanside airport and fortunately was only at about a hundred feet when the engine seized (stopped running and just quit). I had been taught that if you lose an engine on takeoff, do not try to turn back to land again on the runway, continue straight ahead, and pick the softest place to touch down that you could hope for. I landed in some ten-foot-high light brush, landing straight ahead in this canyon that, on the climb out, led straight out over the Pacific Ocean. Thank God that the engine seized where it did and I had not yet climbed out enough to be over the Pacific Ocean. There was no apparent damage to any part of the Piper J-5 aircraft. The mechanic for Oceanside's airport opened the cowling, and we found that the engine had seized and ground to a quick stop while I was barely airborne. He removed one of the lower cylinder spark plugs, and aluminum scrap Babbitt metal fell into his hands. This confirmed that cylinder had eaten its own rings, causing the engine to stop. We got a Jeep and a short rope, and we pulled it back to the mechanic's repair hangar. I quit flying for the day, having just satisfied my instructor that I was ready for the FAA flight exam.

Fifteen minutes after I had my first deadstick landing, I went back to my bachelor officer's quarters (BOQ) and a beer. I took the FAA flight check on May 12 in a Piper J-3 Cub, it went well, and I received my FAA Private Pilot's license.

DEADSTICK LANDING TWO.

Cessna 120 Near a Mountain Lake: I returned to Washington State in the summer of 1946 and continued to fly. I checked out several local airfields and rented Piper Cubs and Cessna 120s. On September 5, 1947, I rented a Cessna 120 (NC1947N) and flew over the Cascade Mountains to Mount Stewart. I was taking geology and needed to take some aerial photographs of the mountain to use for my class. Mount Stewart is 9,415 feet and is one of the largest single pieces of granite in Washington State. I started flying back toward Seattle at about eight thousand feet. The carburetor began running rough, and then my engine stopped. I was about five thousand feet above the terrain. My prop was stopped in a straight-across position. I checked my fuel selector, went through all the checks that I could as I began my five thousand-foot glide back to the mountains below. I dove short distances at a very steep approach angle to try to get the prop to turn over so that I could try force-feeding gas. There were no cleared roads of any size, but I did spot this small lake about one-quarter-mile across. There was a short meadow at the north end that I thought I could land on, but I would go into small brushy trees.

By now I had sixty-eight hours as pilot in command and twenty-three hours of dual for a total of almost ninety-two hours. Gliding south to north, I came in just over the trees on the south end of Fish Lake and used ground effect over the water to touch down on the beach. I landed rolling uphill about one hundred yards and saw that I was going to hit the trees. I hit both brakes and went up and over, landing on the airplane's top, upside down. I was hanging in the seat belt, and I felt liquid on my flight suit. It looked red. I immediately thought that I had been cut badly. Bracing my head, I eased down from being upside down, popped the door, and dropped into the brush. The plane was resting upside down in brush about six feet high. The only damage I could see were dents in the aluminum forward part of the engine cowling. That looked good.

About this time a forest ranger came up in a pickup truck. We found a piece of old telephone wire, hooked it on the tail wheel, and slowly turned the airplane over so it was sitting on its landing gear. I opened the engine cowling and checked the carburetor, and it was dripping water from melting ice. This confirmed my opinion that the engine had quit due to loss of intake air and freezing up of the entry to the carburetor: we call it "carb-heat-ice." In my earlier attempt to restart the engine, I had pulled carb-heat several times, with no success. I started the engine and it ran up just fine. I felt that it was beyond my capability to try to fly it out and opted to have the forest ranger take me to I-90, to a gas station and restaurant to make a phone call to the FAA and close my flight plan. I called the airport owner, a former B-17 pilot and friend, Jim Nordoff. The next morning I drove up with Jim and his aircraft mechanic with some tools and fuel to fly it out. We spotted an eighteen-inch rip in the top fabric on one wing. We found a local miner who kindly gave me an old shirt and a half can of yellow paint. Borrowing a needle and thread, I cut the old shirt into a patch and sewed it onto the wing. I then painted the old shirt a bright yellow and trusted it would get Jim back to the airport in Bellevue. Amazingly, the yellow paint dried pretty quickly and had enough tenacity to be effective as the upper wing surface for the flight back.

To help Jim take off from the very short beach, the mechanic and I towed the tail up inside the trees that had shielded my landing. We had cleared all rocks that might have been hit by the tires on my landing gear. Both the mechanic and I each took a side of the tail horizontal stabilizer and held on, while using the other hand to brace ourselves with the small trees. Jim was running full power, and, when he was ready, he banged his arm on the cabin door and started rolling down to the edge of the beach. He staggered the Cessna 120 into the air, very skillfully, using ground effects, and kept the bird in the air as it was gaining speed. Somehow Jim was able to horse the airplane over the thin Douglas fir trees at the water's edge. He was able to keep the airplane flying down the valley toward I-90 and back to the Bellevue airport. Total cost to pound out the dimples in the aluminum cowling, replace the yellow shirttail fabric on the wing, and finally do a good repair on the carb heat was $440. It was back flying within the week. Jim did not ask for any money as he felt that I had "saved" his Cessna 120 from the fate of being completely destroyed in the central Cascade Mountains. Close examination of the landing gear revealed that upon my landing a rock had sheared the one-quarter- inch copper or aluminum tubing containing hydraulic fluid. That had to be the "blood" that was being dumped on me when I ended upside down in the brush. Other pilots who had rented the same airplane told me that they had troubles with the carb heat as well. It was an accident waiting to happen but it worked out well. There was only minimal damage to the rental aircraft, and because the crash was caused by an aircraft part malfunction, there was no incident report that had to be made to the FAA.

DEADSTICK LANDING THREE

Experimental Bakeng Deuce N54BM: I had been retired nine years from the Marine Corps and had worked as an attorney, law professor, and associate dean for five years when I decided to build my own airplane. It was a Bakeng Deuce high wing, parasol wing, open-cockpit aircraft. I purchased a surplus Lycoming 125 horsepower flat four-cylinder engine, which was used at remote Navy airfields. The Bakeng Deuce was recommended to me by a number of airline pilot friends.

Jerry Bakeng was a local pilot and builder. I purchased a set of plans for forty-five dollars and started building one wing rib per night (there were thirty- two ribs) on a jig on our dining room table. I purchased spruce wing spars from a Tacoma manufacturer and started buying surplus parts from Dick Baxter at Spencer Aircraft near Boeing Field. I did some legal work for Jerry Bakeng, and, in exchange, he welded up the entire fuselage and rudder and horizontal stabilizer. Nine-and-a-half years later, in 1989, I hung everything together and completed the Deuce. I hired one of my law students who was a licensed airframe and power plant (A&P) mechanic and a pilot. Together we completed the aircraft. It had been inspected at various times throughout the nine-plus years by various FAA-designated inspectors. All parts passed construction inspection, and the wings, rudder, horizontal stabilizer, and the aft-half of the fuselage were finally fully covered with fabric. I bought fiberglass cowlings from Jerry and used surplus Boeing Aircraft 737 skin for the forward half of the fuselage. It was a two-seat open-cockpit aircraft. Instruments were obtained from Spencer Aircraft. It was painted in authentic Marine Corps livery, circa 1928, Nicaragua, Royal Air Force (RAF) silver with the traditional "eagle, globe, and anchor," a red squadron leader stripe on the fuselage, and red, white, and blue stars on the wings. The tail was finished with vertical red, white, and blue stripes in historical color and location adherence on the fuselage and wings. Squadron number was VMO-7 and the N-numbers were a regulation black.

Friend Dick Baxter had previously flown Jerry Bakeng's original version of the aircraft so he did the test flights and I started flying off the required thirty hours from the small Issaquah airstrip at the Pickering farm between I-90 and Lake Sammamish. I had flown off the aircraft for its first six hours of flight. I was doing circles at three thousand feet over the Issaquah airport when I noted a high temperature on one of the cylinders. I decided to make a precautionary landing and came in over Lake Sammamish, landing north to south. As I approached the airstrip, a Cessna 180 with jumpers aboard, turned north onto the active runway, without any awareness that I was on final heading for a landing from over Lake Sammamish. I pulled to the right of the landing strip and continued toward I-90 until the jump aircraft was clear and departed. Still at three hundred feet, I applied full throttle to go around to get back on final approach over Lake Sammamish. The Lycoming remained at idle, and I dove to keep my airspeed up. I did a 180-degree turn back north to get over Lake Sammamish again for turn on final. Throttle linkage between my after-rear cockpit flying position to the front cockpit was ineffective. Ahead of me was the Pickering farm, which boarded race horses. I made a last-minute turn left (to the west), slipped through a gap in the poplar trees lining the east side of the runway, and touched down on my landing gear. My plane ended up in a ditch on the west side of the runway. The bolts on the bottom of the fuselage sheared off, and the aircraft continued westbound until the heavy grass and mud slowed it and all forward movement stopped. I was OK; the aircraft was OK except for the bolts in the Cessna landing gear that had sheared off. Their shearing probably saved the aircraft from dropping its nose into the mud, cartwheeling, and turning over.

I loaded the fuselage, with the wings detached, into my pickup truck and drove it to my garage, where we quickly remounted the aircraft on its Cessna spring steel landing gear. It was repaired and ready for more flying off of its thirty hours. The throttle retaining nut and bolt had worked loose, and the Lycoming engine was restarted and run in my driveway, and the replacement linkage worked fine. We towed it to the Snohomish airport on its own landing gear, for additional mechanical tweaking, and it started flying again. The FAA declined to make it an incident because it was registered as an experimental aircraft and there was minimal cost to get it flying again.

CHAPTER 9

Marine Corps Reserve Activity
1946-1951

As I completed active duty during World War II, I was obligated to continue my career in the Marine Corps Reserve. I had the option of completing the three remaining years of five years of commissioned service as a reservist, subject to recall to active duty during that period, or I could contact one of the many Marine Corps Reserve units being established throughout the country. I chose the latter option.

There was the Eleventh Infantry Battalion located in Seattle. I applied to become an active member of that unit. This entailed maintaining certain standards, reporting once a week for drill, and going on active duty for two weeks during the summer months with the unit. The two-week periods took place at Camp Pendleton and usually had some special training such as making an amphibious landing from aboard reserve or regular naval vessels. The aviation components would airlift using Marine Reserve aircraft. These would usually be from Sand Point Naval Air Station in Seattle to either MCAF Camp Pendleton or to North Island NAS in Coronado, California.

Subordinate units of the Eleventh Battalion would meet at different locations. For example, there was an infantry company in Tacoma that it met in the Tacoma Navy Reserve facility, there was a Marine rifle company that met in the Gray's Harbor area, and so on. As I remember, there was a tank unit in Yakima, Washington, and a rifle unit in Spokane. As an infantry officer (MOS 0302), I was assigned as the assault platoon commander; we met and drilled in Seattle with the Eleventh Infantry Battalion at the Navy-Marine Corps Armory. George, although holding an amphibious tractor MOS as his primary, also had kept his 0302 MOS in the Eleventh Infantry Battalion.

Every slot in the battalion was now filled with an infantry-qualified reservist. If the Eleventh Infantry Battalion was recalled (as indeed it was in June 1950), we would travel to Camp Pendleton by troop train (a real war-time experience.). Upon arrival, we would be given quarters and initially live together until each Marine was pulled out and reassigned to a unit requiring their special MOS.

As a reservist, when I was a national park ranger, stationed at Mount Rainier National Park, I would arrange my schedule and drive to Seattle for two days to perform my drill. When I was transferred by the National Park Service to California in the Fresno and later Yosemite National Park areas, I would still drill with the Fresno rifle company as part of the Twelfth Infantry Battalion headquartered in San Francisco, California. I would be assigned to the infantry rifle company located at the Marine Corps Reserve armory located in the Fresno, California area.

In summary, I was released from active duty from World War II in the summer of 1946 and returned to my residence in Bellevue. I entered duty with the Eleventh Infantry Battalion in the Marine Corps Reserve in Seattle, shortly thereafter. Three years from my original commissioning, I was promoted to first lieutenant. I was transferred to the Twelfth Infantry Battalion in September 1948.

Winding Down from Active Duty and Making a Break for the Yukon and Arctic Circle

WHEN I RETURNED TO SEATTLE in 1946, I had five weeks before the fall semester started at the University of Washington. I had always been a fan of the poet laureate of the Arctic, Robert W. Service. His articles and poetry drew many of us to Alaska because of his writing about the Chilkoot Pass, the Trail of 1898, the Yukon, "Cremation of Sam McGee," and other familiar topics.

I got passage north from Seattle to Skagway on the *Princess Louise* in late August. I couldn't get anyone to accompany me, so I went alone. I dressed and packed for a trek into the mountains and rivers of the Yukon. Basically I brought my pack, my ice ax, crampons, and hiking gear. In a Skagway bar, I asked for the location of the entry to the Trail of 1898. It started in a widow's orchard at Dyea, some six miles west of Skagway. The summer of 1946 had seen the passage of nearly fifty years since the trail was last used. Amazingly, I was able to follow the original trail because of the thousands of metal-shorn corked boots that had worn their way into the granite. It was like following a marked trail through the brush and undergrowth.

I was impressed by the debris cast off by the miners as they climbed over the Chilkoot Pass. There were gold pans, small picks and shovels, and sometimes shards of camping gear. When I got to the summit, I hiked about five miles to the tracks of the White Pass and Yukon Railroad. There were no towns or remains of any habitation at the top of the pass, just the railroad tracks winding their way toward Whitehorse, located in the Yukon Territory. I waited beside the track as it ran through the forest. Hearing an approaching train, I stood in the middle of the railroad tracks and waved down a freight train bound for Whitehorse. They took me aboard their "crummy" (caboose) and offered me a beer. It was the best beer I think I have ever had. I joined the train crew, and we ate lunch at a small railroad junction town called Carcross. I had my first caribou steak there with the crew and found it to be excellent.

When we arrived in Whitehorse, I offered to pay my fare, but they refused. I thanked the train crew for their hospitality and sought out the Royal Canadian Mounted Police. The Mounties pointed me in the direction of the steamship offices of the White Pass and Yukon Navigation Company, a subsidiary of the White Pass and Yukon Route rail company. I was asked where I was bound for, and I replied "Fort Yukon and the Arctic Circle." The company worker quickly told me that I could not book passage. The sternwheeler SS *Klondike*, the last passenger sternwheeler, had just made its last run for the season in the fall of 1946.

The SS Klondike.

They would not let me book as a passenger because the sternwheeler was carrying a very large load of dynamite to be dropped at every gold dredge downriver along the Yukon. *Klondike* was temporarily assuming her other role as a cargo carrier. When they carry that much dynamite, regulations prohibit taking on passengers.

Whitehorse is the navigational head of the Yukon River. Yukon means "great river" in Gwich'in and "big river" in Yupik, the two major native languages of the people who live along the northern Yukon passage. The Yukon flows 1,980 miles from Whitehorse, initially north nearly a thousand miles to the Arctic Circle and then swings west for another thousand miles to the Bering Sea in Alaska.

Dismayed but not hopeless, I asked them if they could use a deckhand for the eight- to nine-day run more than 900 miles down the Yukon. They asked about my background, and they seemed impressed that I had served in the Pacific and ended up a Marine lieutenant and that I had also done longshoring in Seattle. They agreed and the *Klondike* became my home for the next week or so.

The *Klondike* was a sternwheeler more than two hundred feet long with a beam of forty feet. As most sternwheelers, she had a shallow draft of two to three feet, which permitted her to travel the river with its widely varying depths of sand bars and riffles. Riffles are defined as shoals, reefs, or shallows in a stream, which produce ripples in the stream surface, quite visible to the ship's pilot, whose navigational high location permits an almost vertical, or lower water level deck, view of the gunwale down to the surface of the river.

There was a single, wood-fired, locomotive-style boiler that fed steam into two high-pressure, single-cylinder, double-acting steam engines mounted longitudinally. These drove the rear paddlewheel by cranks mounted at either end of its axle.

During the Gold Rush, many of the two hundred or so sternwheelers that plied the Yukon River over the years had three decks, as did the *Klondike*. The lower deck was the freight house. Above this, with almost the same dimensions, was the saloon deck carrying most of the vessel's passenger accommodations. Uppermost was the Texas deck with the larger staterooms for the captain, senior crew, and first class passengers. On top of the Texas deck was the small pilothouse. The *Klondike* was later taken out of service, repaired, refurbished, and hauled up on the riverbank in Whitehorse. Today it is used as an arctic museum. Its slightly smaller sister sternwheeler, the *Keno*, was hauled up on the bank in Dawson City, Yukon Territory. Both are popular tourists attractions.

Sternwheelers can't go downriver at night. The pilot, high above the foredeck, can't see the changes in sand bars and riffles after nightfall. He simply pulls to the side of the river and ties up for the night. Natives cut cord wood for the steam boilers.

On the *Klondike*, my job as deck hand was to use a two-wheel dolly and trundle forty to fifty loads of cord wood every night down the gangway. I stacked all of this cord wood on the foredeck, immediately in front of the firebox. The firebox was constantly going and when underway, they force-fed two cords of wood an hour into the glowing red firebox.

The food on the *Klondike* was hearty and good and the crew friendly and helpful. I enjoyed my downriver trip. We passed Lake LeBarge, the location site of the "Cremation of Sam McGee," one of Robert W. Service's most famous poems, and stopped for the night in Dawson and at several other well-known towns along the route. Most of our stops were along isolated portions of the Yukon River bank, frequently at the closest point on the river to where we delivered their share of the dynamite. Upon arrival at Fort Yukon and Circle, I signed off from ship's papers and was free to prowl around.

I could not get a bush pilot until the next day when I then rode with a priest and his sled dogs and a few dredge parts in a DeHaviland Beaver, eventually ending up in Fairbanks.

I was unable to book a hotel room in Fairbanks and turned to the local USO for help. There a lady invited me to sleep on a military cot in their church belfry, which I did until I was able to book a flight to Vancouver, British Columbia, on a DC-3 aircraft. For the seven days waiting for the flight to Vancouver, I worked in the Fairbanks potato harvest, lifting fifty-pound sacks of spuds onto a flatbed truck. I was paid cash ,but I don't remember how much. What kept me going were the two free meals a day in the farmer's house on this farm just outside of Fairbanks.

In sum, it was a great, adventurous trip and confirmed all my dreams of the Gold Rush of 1898. I think Robert Service epitomized how I felt at the time about life and wandering:

The Men That Don't Fit In

There's a race of men that don't fit in,
A race that can't stay still;
So they break the hearts of kith and kin,
And roam the world at will.
They range the field and they rove the flood,
And they climb the mountain's crest
Theirs is the curse of the gypsy blood,
And they don't know how to rest.

A Climbing Ranger and Naturalist

I FLEW TO VANCOUVER, British Columbia, and hitchhiked back to Seattle and my childhood home in Bellevue. I caught up with my family and entered college at the University of Washington (UW) in Seattle, to get my degree in geology, which would qualify me for a position as a ranger naturalist. After two years, I earned a Bachelor of Science in geology, and, in the summer of 1947, I became a ranger naturalist at Mount Rainier and a climbing ranger whenever disaster visited our mountain.

Many of my climbing friends worked as mountain guides for Jim Whitaker's[1] Mt. Rainier Guide Service. During that summer, as a climbing ranger, I made a series of high glacier patrols around the south side of the mountain. We were looking for a crashed Marine transport, a C-46 Curtis Commando, that had crashed on December 10, 1946.

There were thirty-two Marines aboard; all had been missing since the crash. Assistant Chief Ranger Bill Butler, District Ranger Bob Weldon, and I as a ranger naturalist made a series of what were called high glacier patrols. We finally found the wreckage, which had hit the bergschrund of the South Tahoma Glacier at 10,300 feet. The bergschrund is the name given to the highest crevasse on a glacier. It is usually the disconnect between the mass of the glacier and the remaining ice that formed the actual side of the mountain at that elevation. With some help from Army mountain troops' climbers and virtually all of the Mt. Rainier Guide Service (Jim Whitaker's crew), we located all thirty-two Marines bodies.

I was so precise in stating that the elevation was exactly 10,300 feet, because when I climbed into the wreckage, I was in the aircraft cockpit area and pulled the deceased frozen pilot's body back from where it had impacted the instrument panel. Being a pilot, I read the altimeter as a pilot would, and it was pegged at that level by the impact at the time of the crash.

After a host of high glacier patrols to the 10,300 ft. wreckage and agreement from the next-of-kin, the decision was made by the U.S. Navy and the National Park Service to bury all thirty-two Marines in the bergschrund of the South Tahoma Glacier and have memorial services in their memory as closure. It was such a dangerous mission that the lives of rescuers would have been in jeopardy had the mission continued. The South Tahoma Glacier was permanently closed to all glacier climbing, and the Marines rest peacefully in their glacier grave for eternity. Limitations on climbing the South Tahoma Glacier remain.

---

1   Jim Whitaker was the first American to climb Mount Everest.

Recovery team at the site of the crashed Marine transport on the South Tahoma Glacier.

Peacetime and Duty in the Marine Corps Reserve

I COMPLETED my last work at the UW, or so I thought, in 1948. I met and married my wife, Jo-Anne Hopf, (from the Theta sorority) in 1948. I took a summer job as a national park ranger and became the climbing ranger on the north side of the mountain. I handled the majority of mountain climbing accidents for that portion of Mount Rainier. Jo and I lived in a tent-house/cabin at seventy-two hundred feet at Sunrise Park above the Emmons Glacier. At the end of the climbing season in September 1948, Superintendent Preston invited me to apply for a permanent position as a national park ranger. The U.S. Civil Service was going to open the hiring list for consideration to become a national park ranger for the first time since before World War II. I was among the first of fifty selected, and we were off to National Park Service's Millerton Lake just north of Fresno.

My new superintendent, Hugh Peyton, nominated me to attend the NPS-sponsored Federal Bureau of Investigation (FBI) school, which was being held at Yosemite National Park. Jo and I stayed at the ranger club during the school. My instructors in this course were two FBI agents from the San Francisco field office who immediately began trying to recruit me into the FBI. By the second week, the agents were making calls to the FBI headquarters in Washington, DC. They wanted me to come to work for the bureau. Jo and I discussed it very seriously. I had enjoyed myself during the law enforcement aspects of being a national park ranger. I had a number of successful investigations, and I felt that I would like the bureau. At the time, the only way to get into the FBI was with a certified public accountant (CPA) or a law degree. They have since gone back to accepting any university degree, which I feel is a very worthy agent resource.

We came home, and I further discussed the move with mentors whom I respected. They concurred with my decision to resign as a ranger from the NPS, go to law school, and then join the FBI. I called my ranger friends, and they all agreed with my decision. I then resigned from the park service and applied for and was admitted to the University of Washington Law School in Seattle. In June 1950, I had just finished my first year of law school. I was at Camp Pendleton for my active duty reserve training when North Korea invaded South Korea. That signaled my recall as an active member of the Seattle Marine Corps Reserve and ended my law school career for a ten-year interim.

CHAPTER 10

Korean War
1950-1951

When I was recalled to active duty at Camp Pendleton in June 1950, I joined a Marine tank platoon for a very brief period of time. In October 1950, I was selected for special temporary duty (TDY) in Korea as part of an "evaluation team." We were to examine the active duty experience of Marine Corps Reserves who were recalled to active duty and immediately assigned to combat units in Korea. My commander for this specialized duty was Maj. Roland Davis, USMCR, a recalled reservist lawyer from Portland, Oregon. This special duty ran from November 16, 1950, with arrival at Hungnam, North Korea, through my December 21, 1950 return to Camp Pendleton. On January 2, 1951, I was assigned temporarily as commanding officer (CO) Sixth Replacement Draft. I was replaced as CO by a Marine reservist from the midwest, Maj. Foster C. LaHue, shortly after my January assignment.

This was primarily an administrative holding unit to assemble personnel to join replacement drafts of troops to Korea. Following my brief one-month investigative trip to Korea and the First Marine Division in November and December of 1950, Maj. Davis and the other members of our small investigative team reported back on our findings to the Marine Corps. This was done to permit changes in the way infantry training was evaluated. We found a very small group of Marine reservists from southern California who had been recalled and immediately shipped over to

Korea without proper infantry training.

When Maj. LaHue took command of the Sixth Replacement Draft, I became a draft liaison officer until we departed Camp Pendleton for Korea. On the night before our scheduled departure from San Diego's Broadway Pier, we strongly recommended to Maj. LaHue that he not grant overnight liberty to any of the Marines of our Sixth Draft. LaHue overrode our strong recommendation, and he granted overnight liberty. At about 0400 hours, I checked, and we were missing about seventy-five Marines who were scheduled for the 1000 hour sailing from San Diego.

Maj. LaHue was devastated and quickly realized his error in granting overnight liberty to the departing Sixth Replacement Draft. Tijuana was the word the troops had on where our seventy-five missing movement Marines could be found. "Missing movement" is considered one of the most serious crimes that a Marine can commit when under orders for overseas duty.

I took three 6x6 Marine trucks and a jeep, and we hightailed it to the border at Tijuana. I called the Navy border control office and was able to get a Navy lieutenant who was fluent in Spanish.

We explained the situation to the Mexican police manning the border. They directed us to the Tijuana jail. Our missing seventy-five Marines were all in custody in the jail, most for drunk and disorderly conduct.

I explained my request to the jail guard to release the seventy-five Marines to my custody so that we could meet the ship at Broadway Pier in San Diego to make our 1000 hours sailing. I explained that each of these Marines was on orders going into combat in Korea. This made no impression on the Tijuana police. Finally, I threatened to make an "international incident out it and give it to all the press," explaining how the "police at the Tijuana jail would not release the Marines under orders to go into combat."

When I asked how to spell his name for our press release, the police officer in charge suddenly relented and gave me custody of all seventy-five Marines. Still feeling the effects of the cheap Tijuana booze, the hungover Marines were hustled aboard the trucks and we took off for the border. I will mention in passing, that all of the Mexican ladies-of-the-evening who were arrested with our Marines nearly started a riot in the Tijuana jail by piling all of their straw mattresses together and starting a bonfire. This evacuated the jail as we left for the border. Tough foreign jails frequently cause persons incarcerated to commit other crimes. The women starting a jailhouse fire would readily qualify for this classification.

As we crossed the border back into the United States, a California Highway Patrol motorcycle stopped my Jeep and my three-truck convoy. He asked if he could help us

PC 1082 USS Hellhammer

with an escort. He identified himself as a former World War II Marine. He radioed ahead as our sailing time was close approaching. He got a host of California Highway Patrol motorcycle officers, who escorted us with sirens and flashing lights to the foot of Broadway Pier. It was almost like a Randolph Scott Hollywood Marine movie. The ship was just singling up the lines but had not hoisted the gangway yet. We made it in the nick of time, and Maj. LaHue realized we had pulled his missing movement dilemma from the fire. It all ended well.

ALTHOUGH THE SEAS WERE ROUGH on this winter crossing of the Pacific, we made it to Kobe, Japan, reshuffled our gear, and headed for Pusan for off-loading. We went north by train from Taegu, heading for the rear areas of the First Marine Division with our Sixth Replacement Draft of replacements.

By my arrival date in-country (Korea), I had been a lieutenant for six years. With that seniority, I hoped to be assigned as company commander of a rifle company. That was not to happen for about five months. Instead, I was assigned on the division staff to G-2 (intelligence). They were aware that I had just finished my first year of law school and I had a secondary MOS of intelligence officers—my fate was sealed and it became a *fait accompli.*

• • •

Gaining Intelligence by Use of "Line Crossers"

I BECAME THE DIVISION INTELLIGENCE Order of Battle officer. It was my task to keep track of the enemy units to our First Marine Division front, *(i.e.,* Sixty-Sixth Chinese Field Army, etc.). Assistant G-2 Maj. John Babashanian was my boss. He knew that I wanted to get a rifle company in one of the division's regiments. John took me aside and assured me that "in the interim, I can get you out of the CP by having you act as liaison to the Military Intelligence Service Detachment (MISD) line crosser unit." MISD was staffed by Japanese-speaking Americans of Japanese descent (Nisei). As a result of my informal training in spoken Japanese, I had no trouble coordinating with MISD, and we ran a string of South Korean agents to the front of our First Marine Division lines.

We would drop them across the Marine division front lines, dressed in Korean civilian clothes, carrying no cameras or records of any kind. They were to look as much like ordinary Korean refugee citizens as possible. They would cross into enemy territory, go inland about ten miles north and return, noting all unit identifications, road signs, and the like. We would debrief them upon their return. It was helpful that the Japanese I learned as a grade school student aided my understanding of their intelligence gathering. We knew the minute they crossed into enemy territory that they could be taken into custody as prisoners of the Chinese. Knowing this, we took advantage of the fact that many Asian peoples have a fear of the mentally ill. We trained our agents to throw fits and jerk around on the ground, to roll their eyes back, anything to make it appear that they were suffering from some sort of severe mental disorder or neurological affliction. It worked and every time they were taken into custody—they would be released quickly by their Chinese captors and be on their way.

To me, one of the more significant things that happened while running these line crossers was that our line crossers advised me of two wounded U.S. soldiers in a small village to the north of the lines of the Korean Marine Corps (KMC). I chose to try leading a small patrol behind Chinese lines to attempt recovery and rescue of the two wounded U.S. soldiers. That section of our front was very fluid at the time, to say the least. Maj. Babashanian agreed to my plan, and had me flown by chopper to the KMC. I explained my plan to the Korean commander, and he loaned me a squad for my rescue patrol. Basically, we took off after dark, taking with us an American Navy corpsman (who was assigned to KMC). There I was, leading this squad of KMC troopers into Chinese territory. We brought along someone familiar with the village location, and, moving only at night, we got to the village and recovered the two wounded. They had been left behind by their prior Chinese Sixty-Sixth Field Army captors.

We had no stretchers to carry them. As a result of their wounds neither soldier was capable of walking. We used their field jackets, buttoning all buttons and sticking two long thick sticks through the sleeves to carry them out. We joined the bottoms of the two field jackets bottom edge to bottom edge in the center, using very large safety pins from our corpsman's medical pack. We made two stretchers of sorts, and we waited until the next night to return to our lines. We made it back about 0300 hours and fortunately established contact using Korean language, so that we would not be shot coming south into their lines. We used a Jeep ambulance and were able to get medical care for our two wounded soldiers.

Maj. Babashanian was pleased, and the end of my G-2 tour Navy/Marine Corps Letter of Commendation Medal recounted, pretty accurately, what we had done to save those soldiers from behind Chinese lines.

Later, when I returned from Korea and went to work for Brig. Gen. Lewis B. "Chesty" Puller when he was CG Troop Training Unit Pacific, he asked about this "two-day patrol behind Chinese lines." I filled him in since he had not heard about it. Chesty was not prone to casual conversation. I sensed that he liked what he heard, but he said nothing.

CHAPTER 11

Korea: Marine Rifle Company
1951

Having spent about one half of my thirteen-month Korean tour during the G-2 assignment, I was finally made available to join the Third Battalion, Fifth Marines (3/5) as a rifle company commander. Lt. Col. Don Kennedy was my battalion commander, and he had personally requested me. We had become acquainted when he was doing some post-World War II coaching for the Camp Pendleton football team and both my brother and I had played football for him. Our battalion was moving north on the East Coast, above the towns of Yangu and Inje, slightly north of the thirty-eighth parallel. We had been attacking to the north, up a major ridge line that ran north to south up the southern side of Hill 1082, which was approximately three thousand two hundred forty feet high.

My company averaged about two hundred and ten to two hundred and twenty Marines and corpsmen when we moved out. I had some spare machine guns attached to my company from the battalion weapons company, and had my organic 60mm mortar unit. Some days, I would have a forward observer (FO) from our supporting artillery battery, or sometimes an air officer (AO) Marine pilot called a forward air controller (FAC). Frequently, our FAC would be a pilot from one of the main Marine air squadrons that provided our close air support. He would be temporarily working as an FA, and his efforts helped us provide knowledgeable on-the-ground direction for our air support.

When you are assaulting a numerically superior enemy force, up steep terrain, you are under fire from snipers and regular riflemen, subject to both artillery and mortar fire. You have a higher-than-average chance of getting hit. Every one of my officers and I was hit at least once during our tour with H/3/5.

One of my lieutenants was killed shortly after I took command of the company. Second Lt. Joe Sharpe, was a young former captain in the Texas National Guard who wanted to be a Marine officer. He was hit with a shot through his forehead, most probably from a Korean or Chinese sniper. (Marines called this type of head shot "through the horns.")

When you have casualties (every one of our rifle companies did), Marine company commanders always try to write condolence letters to the deceased Marine's next of kin. I always tried to write a letter to the parents, widow if married, or next of kin.

In response to my company commander letter, I received a letter back from Joe Sharpe's father. He told me that he had retired as major in the British Army during WW I and had been wounded eleven times (five times in the Boer War and six times during WW I). He expressed appreciation for my giving him the details of Joe's death, and ended up expressing thanks for officering Joe in the manner that I had. I felt humbled by that letter.

We finally got to the top of the hill we had been fighting for. On the other side of the crest, just forward of my then-position, we had Chinese troops in kapok padded uniforms, and they were freezing in the cold temperatures. We had begun to get snow at night, and we had been fighting in the snow up the hill as we progressed. About this time, we had a change in battalion commanders—Lt. Col. Don Kennedy finished his tour and left for the States. His replacement was Lt. Col. Barney McLean, who came right on board and proved every bit as experienced, aggressive, and supportive as Don Kennedy had been.

Lt. Col. McLean called me on his radio and told me to "stop any further movement north." This was December 1951. He advised that my front lines were "now the trace of what is going to be called the demilitarized zone (DMZ)." By map, we were still slightly north of the Thirty-eighth parallel. Years later, I was invited back by the Korean government to be recognized for my actions. I came back, and after the memorial services that were held for the most part in Western Korea, near Seoul, I had gotten a rental car, and with one of my former Korean interpreters as a guide, we located an approach to the DMZ that was just south of where my rifle company had been told to stop. On this return to the area visit, I could not help but notice that our rifle company's area on the DMZ had become the commercial ski area of the eastern side of Korea. The area was loaded with ski lodges and ski slopes.

Of the twenty-seven Marine rifle companies in Korea at that time, three were commanded by senior first lieutenants like me (I had been a lieutenant more than six years at that time), and the remaining twenty-four rifle companies were each commanded by Marine captains. I had commanded the rifle company for five months in combat, and we had our share of fire fights and incoming.

Barney had a fairly senior captain who was eager to take my place as company commander. He brought me back from my company, and I went back to the command post, assuming the job as S-2 intelligence officer for our battalion. After five months of command of this rifle company, I was torn by angst for my Marines and corpsmen. About two weeks after leaving the rifle company, the Red Cross contacted 1stMarDiv and recommended that they send, George, then an Amtrac platoon commander in Inchon, and me back to the States immediately. Our mother was dying. We made it home just before she died. I felt closure in this part of my life.

I was flown off the lines by a Bell helicopter down to a small grass airstrip on the East Coast. I watched a C-54 carefully land on this grass airstrip to pick me up. They flew me to Tokyo, and I flew out the next day on a Canadian RAF transport non-stop into Vancouver, British Columbia. Three hours later I made it to the hospital, the day before she died. It felt good to be back with my wife and "life was good."

JO HAD BEEN LIVING with her parents at their family home. I had been gone about thirteen months. To have a little bit of time alone with each other, we went to a movie. I did not notice even the name of the movie as we entered the theater. It was a picture about World War II, *The Battle of El Alamein,* a famous desert battle between German Gen. Erwin Rommel and British Gen. Bernard Montgomery in North Africa. It was complete with the actual recorded sound track of the battle.

As the first German 88s, a high-velocity German artillery fire, came toward the cameraman, I involuntarily dropped to the floor in a prone position seeking cover among the theater's seats. It was obvious that the five days since helicoptering from the front lines had not been enough time to keep my body from reacting to the sounds of combat. We left the theater. Jo had been quite shaken by my body's involuntary reaction to the reality of the sound track. In all probability, my body would again react precisely in the same way today, courtesy of thirteen months in Vietnam and a later complete diagnosis of PTSD—Post Traumatic Stress Disorder—according to my two psychiatrists from the Veterans Affairs hospital.

My return from Korea, probably a week or so earlier than a routine end-of-tour rotation, moved me up for a change-of-duty transfer. After some post-combat leave in Seattle with Jo's parents, we loaded our single (no children yet) convertible with all of our worldly goods (not many at that point) and headed south to Coronado, California, directly across Mission Bay from San Diego.

CHAPTER 12

Amphib Recon School and "Chesty" Puller
1952-1954

I reported in to Troop Training Unit Pacific (TTU Pac). It was a school for the training of both U.S. troops and foreign troops from our allies including Korean Marines and Army units, Chinese troops from Taiwan, Thai troops from Thailand, and others. Each year TTU Pac would deploy teams of instructors for five to six months (with equipment and training aids that were mobile) to overseas locations. We usually went to Yokuska, Japan, and operated from there to other bases throughout Southesat Asia.

My initial CG was Brig. Gen. Jack Davis, who was shortly replaced by Gen. "Chesty" Puller. Initially, Gen. Davis had me doing general instructing on amphibious operations. When Chesty arrived, he apparently liked to have short talks with his new officers. He reviewed my brief WW II commissioned career as a combat swimming platoon commander and asked what I had learned from that duty. I replied I learned how to land reconnaissance teams from submarines to gather information. We then talked about Korea. He seemed interested that I had helped run a string of agents, the line crossers, to get information for our Marine division. Surprisingly, he asked me what I had done between WW II and the Korean War. I told him that I had gone back to finish my last year of college, but that did not seem to impress him. However, when he found out that I was a climbing ranger and had done some law enforcement work, he became more interested. He was apparently impressed that I continued to fly as an active general aviation pilot as a hobby and had built my own diving helmet when I was younger. Chesty assigned me to be the officer-in-charge (OIC) of the Marine Corps' reconnaissance school.

I was blessed with two assistant instructors, Lieutenants Dana Cashan and Bob "Mumbles" Maiden, both of whom came from reconnaissance backgrounds. I picked up a lot from both of them. About this time, I made a good friend in newly promoted Maj. Kenny Houghton, former commanding officer of the recon company of First Marine Division, who had bravely swum across the Han River under heavy fire, with his then-Sgt. Ernie DeFazio after the Inchon Landing in 1950. While technically still under treatment at Yokosuka Naval Hospital after being hit by artillery fire while crossing the Han, Ken volunteered for recon operations behind the lines along the east coast of Korea from the submarine USS *Perch*.

After several weeks with the recon school, Chesty called me in and asked for my thoughts on recon in the Marine Corps. I candidly told the general, that I thought the Marine Corps was still trying to use World War II tactics, equipment, and methods for a much-changed Marine Corps because of the atomic battlefield. He asked me, "What can we do?" I advised that there were better ways to get our commanders better intelligence, more rapidly, using newer methods of insertion. I told him that we should have small teams, trained in parachuting, that would be capable of jumping from jet aircraft launched from an aircraft carrier. I added that although our use of submarines worked in WW II, there were better methods and equipment that would not make our submarines as vulnerable once they surfaced. I told Chesty that we should develop the new methods and equipment as soon as possible.

I remember Chesty asking a final question: "Has anyone done these things that you are suggesting?" I told him, "No, not at this time, but I am confident that we can develop all of these things that I have been telling you about."

Chesty replied, "I believe you." He then told me to go home to my Coronado apartment, sit down, and write up everything that I had told him, and that he would send it to Gen. Lem C. Shepard, USMC Commandant. I did as asked, and he followed through with the Underwater Dive Team (UDT) Commandant.

I QUICKLY BEGAN to upgrade my personal qualifications for my new duties. Chesty sent me to UDT Dive School. I then did a number of joint submarine operations with the UDT teams, operating from a number of different submarines, USS *Perch*, USS *Ronquil*, and USS *Bream*. Later Chesty sent me on temporary assignment to Naval Air Station (NAS) North Island for some parachute training.

I learned to "whip silk" (as it is called by Navy/Marine Corps riggers), meaning that I learned to pack parachutes. I then made five free-fall jumps with the parachutes that I had packed. We jumped at Camp Elliot, just east in the foothills of San Diego. I had the good sense to carry reserve parachutes that had been packed by highly experienced parachute riggers.

I made two deployments to Japan and Korea, instructing in both locations. It was good experience, and we worked as teams instructing the U.S. Army and, on occasion, Japanese forces. During my tour with Gen. Puller, my amphibious recon school ran two recon schools for Marines from Camp Pendleton. One was for Maj. "Stormy" Sexton for another Marine recon unit. I also ran a two-week course for Navy beach jumpers that entailed teaching land recon techniques to these operators whose skills were in deception used in conjunction with normal amphibious landings.

We learned much ourselves in providing these two Marine courses, and we gained from our interaction with the beach jumpers, particularly in operating from their Navy PT boats in an operation that we ran with them out on San Clemente Island off the California coast.

During these two-plus years, I became more knowledgeable and far more qualified as a Marine diver, operating from submarines. Thus, I had to conclude that even though we were the instructors, we came away from this period far more qualified ourselves.

Gen. Puller was very complimentary of the high-quality training that he had received while attending Army advanced infantry training at Fort Benning, Georgia ,in 1931. His instructors at the advanced infantry course read like a "Who's Who" of WW II senior generals: Generals George Catlett Marshall and George Patton, to name just two. His Marine Corps classmates at Fort Benning included Captains Gilder Jackson, Oliver P. Smith, and 1st Lt. Gerald Thomas, all of whom, along with Chesty, became Marine general officers.

At the end of my tour at OIC Recon School, Chesty asked the commandant, Gen. Shepherd, to assign me to the advanced infantry course at Fort Benning. I had completed parachute and jumpmaster training with Army Airborne. Our class at Benning was about ninety percent West Pointers, and I got along well with them. Later at Khe Sanh, the G-3 of First AirCav, in their relief operation up Route 9, was a classmate from Fort Benning, Col. Collier Ross, who became an Army three-star, commanding the Sixth Army at the Presidio.

CHAPTER 13

Fort Benning, Georgia
1954-1955

I was delighted to be selected for the advanced infantry course at Fort Benning, a class of about ninety Army officers and ten foreign officers from England, China, Turkey, and several South American countries. That year there were just two Marines selected for the course, Maj. Frank Caldwell and myself. Nearly every one of the ninety Army officers was from the West Point classes of 1945 through 1950.

With the exception of the ten foreign officers, virtually everyone in this class had been in combat. Most were captains and had served as company commanders for at least half their tours and the other half in battalion, regiment, and division staff positions. Silver Stars and Purple Hearts, with a smattering of Bronze Stars, appeared among the standard decorations for these Army officers. All were friendly to us, although we were a little put off by the delineation of Frank and me on the training schedules. First, besides the two of us Marines, everyone in the class was either a West Pointer or distinguished military graduate (DMG) from some of our finer universities, followed by the ten foreign officers. Frank had been a Marine company commander at Iwo Jima during World War II, so his Navy Cross set him apart from the rest of us who had served as company commanders in combat.

The thing that rather gave us a twinge was Frank's and my inclusion on all of the training schedules using our designation as "Foreign Officers or U.S. Marines." We got back at them a bit when we ate hot mess hall lunches. There were always a number of enlisted who were instructor assistants or who brought out the food. Frank and I would watch all of the West Pointers, in particular, race to the head of the chow line. The two of us always made it a point to hang back until all the enlisted had been served and then we would go through.[1] A few of our West Point classmates got the message, and they would also wait with us until all enlisted had been served. The foreign officers observed this also, and I believe we Marines went up in their esteem as a result.

Most of the instruction appeared to be aimed at future regimental, brigade, or division commanders. Frank and I would respond in the expected division level response, but in our minds was the reality that when we got back to the FMF, we would be in leadership roles in mostly battalion or regimental positions. It worked fine, and we enjoyed the outstanding talent of the tactics instructors. I had only one disagreement with the instructional staff and that was to a presentation by an Air Force lieutenant colonel. He made a presentation to bring us all up to speed on a review of our complete inventory of every aircraft flown by the U.S. from World War II to the current. I had been warned by Marine seniors to try to maintain a low profile. This air force instructor's omission was more than I could take. I politely asked why he had omitted a single engine aircraft that could carry more bombs than the B-17 at a higher speed with one tenth of the crew requirements. He quickly attacked my question and loudly told the class there was no such aircraft.

At the morning coffee break, I headed immediately to the Fort Benning technical library, two floors down. I quickly photocopied two pages from *Janes (All the World) Aircraft of the World*. At the end of the break, I quietly approached the air force instructor and asked if he would like to see the information that I had found for him. He turned me down and insisted that I share my information with our entire class. I then proceeded to tell the class about our Navy Douglas AD6, which bested the latest model Boeing B-17G Flying Fortress in speed, tonnage of bombs, and confirming it had a crew of one versus the Boeing ten-person crew. The only thing that the B-17 bested the AD on was altitude; 18,000 feet for the AD6 versus 25,000+ on the Boeing B-17. The air force instructor, I must say, was a true gentlemen and he apologized profusely on his lack of knowledge of the AD. He became a good friend as the year-long class continued. In the end, it did not appear to hurt me being thought of as a know-it-all. I ended up finishing in the top ten of our class. By finishing in the top ten, I had apparently bumped one of the West Pointers from doing a one-year tour anyplace and then being automatically assigned to Army Command and Staff

---

1 There is a tradition in the Marine Corps that officers do not eat until all enlisted have been served.

College, with a sure promotion to major. The majority of the West Pointers in our class were very gracious in recognizing that one of their two Marines had beaten out one of their West Point classmates.

SPRING CAME, and I was running daily and doing many push-ups and pull-ups in preparation for Army airborne instruction as a jumper and jumpmaster. I passed all, and we had orders to go to the west coast at Camp Pendleton to Marine Corps Test Unit One. I had no idea what that assignment entailed, but I was ready.

In closing on Fort Benning, I felt that as Chesty had promised from his experience in 1932, "The instruction you will find is super, and you will make many friends whom you will run across the rest of your service life." Chesty was right. Years later I ran into Chesty when I had the Med battalion, and he signed one of his bulldog-appearing pictures and personalized it to me. I believe that generosity was from the guidance that I used to seek from him and the memories of his time at Fort Benning.

CHAPTER 14

Experimental Test Unit One
1955-1957

Having three years in rank as a captain, I was then promoted, at age thirty, to major and assigned to Marine Corps Test Unit One at Camp Pendleton, California. In this experimental unit, which was purposely formed outside of the FMF, we developed new tactics and procedures for use on a potential nuclear battlefield. I became chief research officer and project officer for reconnaissance in the Marine Corps. We formed and trained recon parachutists while developing new methods of entry into and out of submerged submarines.

Becoming Qualified as Test (Experimental) Parachutists

WE LEARNED TO FREE FALL from jets and operationally started routinely jumping from jet aircraft launched from carriers. Many of us became qualified test parachutists and pioneered a number of new aircraft in support of parachute reconnaissance, the F3D and A3D from Douglas Aircraft, the North American AJ1 Savage, and the S2F from Grumman.

The Naval Parachute Unit, located at Naval Air Facility (NAF) El Centro, California, trained its own experimental test parachutists. Chief instructor in this specialized course was CWO Lew Vinson, a highly qualified parachutist in his own

Navy Douglas A3D carrier-based bomber, which was used to drop four- to six-man parachute recon teams, using bomb bay exit.
Photo Courtesy of Boeing/Douglas Aircraft.

right. He and several of his instructors had developed a twenty-two-jump syllabus to obtain this qualification.

The course began with a series of free-fall exits—with varying delays of ten, fifteen, twenty, twenty-five, and more second delays of free falls from the time of exit to the time of scheduled opening. These were a mix of day jumps and night jumps, all from a variety of different types of aircraft.

OVER THE NEXT FEW YEARS, while perfecting and testing the parachute elements of our new recon in the Marine Corps, our duty at Naval Auxiliary Air Facility (NAF), which was smaller in size than a designated NAF, led us to parachute from every service's aircraft. In an ecumenical manner, we jumped from the following aircraft by service: Navy P2V Lockheed Neptune bombers, Navy Grumman TF-1 "Trader," Navy Grumman "Skynight" F3D2 jets (Marine Corps F3D2s), Navy North American AJ-2 "Savage" (combination turbo-prop and jet), Air Force C-47 Douglas "Skytrains," Air Force Fairchild C-119, "Flying Box Cars," Air Force C-123 "Providers," and a U.S. Army De Havilland "Beaver" L-20. These were eight distinct and very different aircraft.

Naval Auxiliary Air Facility, located at El Centro, had other services that were provided by their staff, and they were able to develop information and techniques from those respective services. Capt. Larry Neipling was an Army jumper, and we exchanged parachuting information with their facilities at Fort Benning and Fort Bragg. In a like manner to the diverse types of aircraft listed above, we had air force testing information from the 6511th Aero Test (parachute) squadron at Edwards AFB, California, in the desert. CWO Larry Lambert, USAF, was their point person on all testing being done there and at Edwards AFB. They kept us current with what the Air Force was doing at Wright-Patterson AFB, Ohio.

As the reconnaissance and pathfinder project officer, I was blessed by getting Capt. Joe Taylor, a Naval Academy graduate who came from commanding the Third MarDiv Recon Company. He became my reconnaissance exec. We had a few recon Marines, and they came under Joe's and my recon experience. We later joined First Lt. Don Koelper, who quickly took over our "pathfinding project," later gaining the term of honor, "Mr. Pathfinder." All was not just parachute development. We gained some very experienced divers for Captains DeFazio and Bill McKinstry as the amphib recon leaders of our combat swimming platoon, and they were soon joined by a number of experienced swimmers and divers. They were Sergeants Robert "Guts" Guttierrez, Bobby J. Patterson, and Milt Runnels. Collectively, they all made our swimmer group of developers shine. All became gunnery sergeants as their experience and performance quickly dictated pathfinding in the Corps.

Following the developmental work being done—first at Test Unit One, and then, later, within the force recon companies—this all led to the development and use, including in combat, of reconnaissance pathfinders in our Corps.

When first assigned to Marine Corps Test Unit One, my new commanding officer, Col. Ed Rydalch, and his executive officer, Lt. Col. Regan Fuller, kept reminding all of us of the many issues that were assigned to our developmental mission. How could we help in changing the Marine Corps to better serve the country in performance of our mission?

Most of us initially took a fairly narrow approach to our respective portions of the overall mission. I credit two of our officers at Test Unit One with breaking us free of our initial narrow approach. Our commandant, Gen. Shepard, tried to assemble both thinkers and doers who were experienced commanders and operators from various disciplines and activities within the Marine Corps. He chose Col. Rydalch as an accomplished colonel who had the intellect to foresee the tactical and equipment improvements on the horizon that would cause us each to examine these issues from the diversity of our respective experiences. Many of us were field-grade officers with a host of backgrounds. Two aviators assigned to our group, Maj. Claude "Barney" Barnhill and Maj. "Red Dog" Jernigan, were both experienced fighter pilots and outstanding Marine aviators. They were well respected by their seniors and juniors alike. They were a great help to us in pathfinding.

Marine aviation in the early 1950s was expanding rapidly, and our command leadership was envisioning regimental-sized helicopter landings, with greater "in from the beach" distances. Keep in mind that ground positioning satellite (GPS) navigation had not been fully developed yet. Our guidance on the battlefields of the future: operate with greater distances than what we had operated in the past. Our next war-to-be in Vietnam had not developed yet. We were still using helicopters without complete air superiority, such as we did later during the war in Vietnam. Helicopter pilots wanted to stay low in their final approach to touchdown to avoid enemy defensive weapons that were 12.7mm /50 caliber. Navigation of helicopters at relatively low "nap of the earth" altitudes (50-150 feet) is very difficult. Suggestions on use of "navigation assist fixed wing" were discussed and tried. Test unit officers were very aware of the Army's use of ground guidance by the pathfinders that the Army used in all of its airborne assaults. Working with the helicopter squadrons from our air wing at El Toro, Marines from both ground and air became very innovative. Capt. Taylor and now-promoted Capt. Koelper and I (as a major), had all trained as pathfinders when we went through Fort Benning. With our lead helicopter operator, Lt. Col. William "Bill" Mitchell, from El Toro, each of us at Test Unit One began to develop the idea of parachuting pathfinder teams into a designated helicopter landing zone (LZ) with guidance gear and radios to solve the low-approach-altitude problems of helicopter navigation. It worked from the start and there was input from both sides so that we ensured mutually compatible capability.

Parachute insertion about twenty to thirty minutes prior to the scheduled landing began to be used on both coasts. After splitting First Force and sending off half of the jumpers and divers, the helicopter units from the Second Military Airlift Wing (MAW) and Second Force Recon established the same close relationship, and all of the East Coast helicopter landings used the same tactics and equipment. In addition, all teams carried aircraft-compatible radios (MAY and AN/GRC9).

In closing this brief overview of Marine Corps' pathfinding, it is of interest to note the last-known combat use of pathfinders guiding in helicopter landings was during our invasion of the Dominican Republic in 1965. Both the helicopters and the Marine pathfinders from Second Force Recon took casualties. Despite their collective losses, the landings went well, and the enemy was defeated on a contested battlefield. First Lt. Ken Taylor and his team of pathfinders set up the LZ at Haina Port, west of Santa Domingo. After the successful evacuation of all of the landing force, a meritorious mast was held on the USS *Boxer* (LPH), and that ended pathfinding in the Marine Corps as we knew it in those days. Within a year, developments and usage of small GPS units used by both the landing troops and by the helicopters began. Pathfinders became excess to the needs of the Corps and were disbanded and reassigned within the respective recon units.

CHAPTER 15

Forming of First Force Recon Company
1957-1959

In 1957, we formed First Force Recon Company within the Fleet Marine Force, and I was assigned as the founding CO. The next year, I sent half of my divers and jumpers back to Camp Lejeune to form Second Force Recon under my former exec, Maj. Joe Taylor, and his exec, Maj. Paul Xavier "P.X." Kelley, who was later the twenty-eighth commandant of the Marine Corps. They continued development in both parachuting and diving in Second Force Recon in the Second Marine Division at Camp Lejeune. USS *Sealion* was their go-to submarine in all of their water work.

First Force Recon Company deployed overseas, and we successfully supported a two-division Marine landing in the Philippines jungle, under the soon-to-be new Commandant Gen. David Shoup. During the Vietnam War, a total of six force recon companies were formed within the Fleet Marine Force, five of which served in-country with great success. One company was left in the States as a source for when the Marines needed to man the other five companies.

A parachute problem arose with the former parachutists from the World War II Marines who had served in the paramarines (Marine paratroopers). The problem was that most of the former paramarines had become fairly senior (as majors and lieutenant colonels). When we began parachuting, they began to voice disagreement with my Test Unit One parachutists and later when I formed and became first commanding officer of First Force Recon. They would come in and express undue concern about our tactics and methods of operation.

The paramarines were established in the Corps in 1942, jumping mostly on the West Coast at Camp Elliot and San Diego and later at Camp Pendleton, California. They never made a combat jump. They fought bravely and with great distinction as an elite infantry, but they were disbanded in 1944. They were put into the Marine Corps Fifth Division (V Div), which became one of the most distinguished of the six divisions that fought in World War II, primarily at Iwo Jima. As a major myself, I offered to give them some indoctrinal briefings, but they refused my help. They reminded us that they "were jumping out of airplanes before you were commissioned." I have to say, as a thirty-year-old major, I did not care for being called a "youngster." I had more time in combat, thirteen months of continuous combat, as a Marine rifle company commander and running a string of intelligence spies than any of them with their two-plus years of intermittent combat during World War II. In my objective opinion, I could understand their interest, but they knew absolutely nothing about the sophisticated parachuting that we had developed. They knew nothing about free-fall parachuting, and jet planes were ten years past their two years of jumping experience ending in1944. After experiencing their unfounded derision in briefings about our operations, I went to Gen. Shoup, our division commander, and explained our frustration with the unwanted derision that we were getting from these older, former paramarines. He had noticed this himself and came up with a solution. He designated me CO of First Force Recon, to be his "staff parachute officer." Thereafter, any comments that were offered about parachuting had to come through me. That immediately stopped for good their negative comments.

Gen. Shoup was very perceptive, and he was aware of the highly skilled help that we were getting from the Naval Test Parachute Center and their staff. He was fully aware of the distinction between the technology from twenty years before and the then-current, more sophisticated, experimental, and free-fall parachuting that we had developed and become proficient in. Later, we gave several of the brighter old-timers complete briefings. They were satisfied that our current crop of parachutists were fully competent and innovative as well, thus ending the negative comments from them.

We jumped with several different types of parachutes in our experimental work: the "QFB" (quick fit back), the "QAC" (quick attachable chest) pack, backpacks, chest packs, seat packs, and conicals. The conical was a small, twenty-six-foot chute named for its unusual shape. Our usual chute for jumping with weapons and equipment was a T-34 airborne/paratrooper parachute. Thus, jumping with the very small twenty-six-foot parachute gave us a much faster rate of descent, whereas the T-34 was a much lower speed drop that reduced injuries from jumping with equipment. Many of our test chutes were shaped in an oblate spheroid. If one took an inflated basketball and cut the bottom third off, that's what an oblate spheroid looks like. The suspension lines appear to attach to the bottom of the chute. Actually, the suspension lines run in one continuous line of parachute cord from the bottom on one side, up over the top center, and down the opposite side. This construction provides a very strong suspension line pattern that adds greatly to the strength of the parachute.

Each of us was required to jump once in the pressurized "space suit." It had a large screw-on Plexiglas® helmet, which had a metal ring-to-ring attachment system. The neck of the space suit had a metal ring like a large bottle cap. The space helmet had a similar metal ring that fit on top of the suit's ring. One rotated the helmet about one-eighth turn and locked the helmet onto the neck ring of the space suit. There were metal pressure rings at each wrist as well. Most of us felt a bit uncomfortable in the space suit because the parachutist had difficulty unlocking, turning, and lifting off the helmet. I personally could not bend my arms in the space suit; I had to be able to get my hands up to rest on the space suit helmet to unlock it. I made sure to slip my canopy to land as close as possible to the corpsmen in our safety ambulance on the landing zone. The space suits were of varying sizes and the one I was issued was for a person six feet tall—I was six feet three inches tall.

We jumped with so many different kinds of parachutes, most of which had the ripcord located in a different place, that we had to pause just before jumping to remind ourselves where this ripcord was so that we could pull it properly.

Author preparing for the first operational reconnaissance parachute jumps from a Grumman F3 Carrier jet, 1957.

Each of us had made over a hundred parachute jumps by the time we finished our experimental parachuting. The casual observer might think that we were "stacking the numbers" to build up our jump logs. That was not the case. We found that after you do about ten jumps, your body and mind become much more attuned to the jumping process. It was as if our minds had slowed down and we were able to evaluate what our body positions were, where the aircraft was at time of exit, and like observations. Post-jump questioning and interviews became experimental debriefings by the two NPU[1] parachute engineers, Howard Fish and Ken Earle. We continually exchanged information on our experimental parachuting with the Army units parachuting at Fort Benning, and with the air force at Wright Patterson AFB. Capt. Joe "Kitt" Kittinger, USAF,[2] came out on temporary duty to El Centro when we were doing some of our experimental jumps, and he jumped several times with us. In Vietnam, Kitt, then a lieutenant colonel, was shot down, and he spent time in a Vietnamese prison.

A former classmate from the Advanced Infantry School at Fort Benning, West Pointer Army Capt. Clint Norman, arranged an invitation for me to go Fort Bragg. Clint was now in special forces and was heavily involved at Fort Benning with developmental work using parachutes. I felt comfortable associating with other persons using parachute entry for their particular special operations. I ensured that my former executive officer Capt. Taylor, then serving as CO of Second Force Recon at Camp Lejeune, was also invited. We had other participants, from the Central Intelligence Agency (CIA), USAF Col. Harry "Heinie" Aderholt's[3] air commandos, and ourselves as the Marine Corps reps. While at Fort Bragg, Norman introduced me to a distinctive U.S. Army Special Forces officer, Maj. Lucien E. "Lew" Conein. As a young lieutenant at the close of WW II, Lew had parachuted into Indochina (now Vietnam) as part of Wild Bill Donovan's Office of Strategic Services (OSS) fight against the Japanese. After his jump, Lew was wounded and taken to a Vietnamese village where he was nursed back to health by the chief of the village's seventeen-year-old daughter, Ellyette. The romantic part of that story was that upon repatriation at the end of WW II, he immediately flew back to that village and married Ellyette, his wife to this day.

After a few adult beverages with Clint and Lew, I couldn't help but notice Lew had two fingers missing on his hand. I presumed that it was a result of some Vietcong ambush when on his OSS mission. He leveled with me, and the true story was that

---

1 Naval Parachute Unit
2 After he made a balloon drop from 102,800 feet, Kitt held the Guinness World Record for the highest free-fall parachute jump. That altitude record held until 2013.
3 Harry C. Aderholt retired as a Brigadier Gen.. He passed away at age 90 in 2010.

he was helping the proverbial little old lady here in the United States who had car trouble. Before he started, he cautioned her not to hit the starter while he was doing his repair. She did it anyway and the fan belt took off his two fingers. Parachutists are not immune from what some call gallows humor. Lew picked up the trooper name of "three-finger Louie." Missing two fingers did not deter his weaponry prowess in the least. Lou was heading the Army HALO (high altitude, low opening) developmental parachute insertion program. Having done quite a bit of experimental jumping in our own HALO program, I told Lew about Sgt. Zwiener's and my jumps from jets at 25,000 feet. He was stunned and was unaware of the depth of our developmental research. I immediately invited Lew to El Centro, and he jumped out of the Grumman TF-1.

Of course, we then checked him out, and he jumped the Douglas F3D2 carrier jet. From that moment on, the Marine Corps Recon and the Army HALO program began exchanging all kinds of information, thus speeding up both of our respective programs.

Knowing Lew's proficiency in French and in Vietnamese, I was not surprised to find out that Lew was the last-reported American seen with President Ngo Dinh Diem and his brother (Ngo Dinh Nhu), who were killed in the back of a Vietnamese armored personnel carrier (APC) in Saigon in November 1963. Lew was supposedly "the carrier" of the $40,000 reportedly paid to the alleged cabal of South Vietnamese generals by the United States for the assassination of President Diem and his brother.

• • •

Buoyant Ascents: First Time Used from U.S. Submarines

THE DIVER HALF of First Force Recon was busy as well, pushing the envelope on modifications for our work with submarines. We continued to conduct sub ops, many times alone, sometimes with UDT[4] units, in support of west coast landings. My former exec, Capt. Taylor, started continuing developmental operations at Camp Lejeune in Second Force Recon. Both units were working on making periscope tows. Our submariners from Submarine Flotilla One continually made us aware of the submarine vulnerability when operating on the surface. They wanted us to continue to develop ways to reduce the surface time on their submarines and improve our surface periscope tows. To cut down our surface time, we began to use the doghouse, the after stowage area, in the after conning tower structure, to keep our inflatable boats more inflated, thus reducing the surface time required for past launchings.

---

4   Underwater Demolition Team, Navy Seals.

We configured tow hookup points on a line that we placed in front of the conning tower. The sub would surface, all divers equipped with Self Contained Underwater Breathing Apparatus (SCUBA) gear would exit, and the submarine would submerge with each of the divers hooked onto a "D" ring with all of the other divers. The submarine would tow us in, bottom-depth permitting, to unhook from the periscope tow-line, complete their mission, and then rendezvous with the sub.

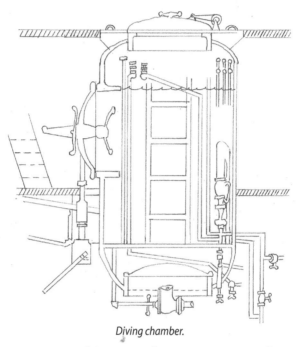

Diving chamber.

In our continuous review of German submarine operations from World War II, I became aware of the German usage of "buoyant ascent" from their sunken subs. It was a new and different way to escape rather than using a rebreather or other means of escape. Buoyant ascent is the technique whereby a diver with just a face mask, fins, and a swimsuit is equipped with a specially designed Mae-West life jacket with air valves permitting deflation (exhaling during ascent). Thus the diver can exhale, let go of the sub, and, using the buoyancy of the Mae West jacket, go to the surface as a normal recon surface swimmer.

I asked our diving medical officer (DMO) if we could possibly use the buoyant ascent technique to ascend from a submarine that remained submerged. He agreed that this could work, but he wanted my divers and me to go through the submarine escape tower at Pearl Harbor to become comfortable using buoyant ascent. I detail this technique in my first book, *Fortune Favors the Brave* (Chapter 10, pp.158-179).

We began to prepare for the development of buoyant ascent to an operationally accepted technique for entry through training during the remainder of 1957 and early 1958. I took Capt. DeFazio, First Lt. Bill Mckinstry, and nine enlisted divers to Pearl Harbor. We did nothing but practice buoyant ascents and chamber re-entries by "skinning it in" for a week. In August 1958, we did the first ever buoyant ascents from a U.S. submarine bottomed at 110 feet off the Del Coronado Hotel in San Diego without any problem. We performed day and night buoyant ascents and then repeated the same once underway, day and night, clean with no gear and then later dirty with full equipment. No problems arose. CNO and CMC did insist on placing a submarine rescue vessel, the ASR *Chanticler*, moored overhead of USS *Perch*, but we never needed her. *Chanticler* was fully equipped for dive support. She had a recompression chamber that CNO's office wanted to have overhead as we made the first-ever operational buoyant ascents from a U.S. Navy vessel.

Initially, we used small lock-in bottles to take our divers from the surface down thirty-four feet to the open escape trunk. We would enter, blow the escape trunk free of seawater after securing the outside sea hatch, then just re-enter the forward torpedo room. Each of my nine enlisted divers and officers DeFazio, McKinstry, and I had been "skinning it in" at fifty feet in the tower. ("Skinning it" is a term meaning diving without an air bottle or other air assist.) None of us needed to use a lock-in bottle, so we could put more recovering divers into the trunk and get all hands back aboard, with the submarine not once having to surface during the whole exercise. We had made a lot of progress in better utilization of submarines. Later, we performed numerous recoveries into submerged submarines. All of this experimental work was done four years before the SEALs (Sea, Air, Land teams) came into existence. When we began to intensify our use of submarines, trying to stay submerged, great emphasis was placed on finding the submarine once our missions on land or off the beaches were completed.

The "Beany" Failed in Helping "Find the Submarine"

FORCE RECON WORKED CLOSELY with the Naval Undersea Lab located on Point Loma, San Diego. They had come up with an "infrared" device to help us find the submarine, called the "Beany." We called it the "Beany" because it looked like the device that a child's TV program of the time entitled "Beany" was called. It fit on top of the diver's helmet and would emit a signal to help us locate the submarine on its underwater approach to recover swimmers. Despite its technical promise, from the

Author doing the first operational buoyant ascent from USS Perch *(APSS-313) August 25, 1956, from 110 feet.*

practical standpoint it was found to be unusable. Our divers were ingesting too much water, swimming on the surface, and having to continually turn and aim" the "Beany" to find the submarine. We thanked the lab, and chose to pursue other possibilities.

We finally determined that it was beyond our Marine divers' capabilities or equipment for us to find the submarines. We asked for help from the submariners. They told us that they could find us. Their sonars with their highly qualified operators could locate a click when we tapped our K-Bar dive knives against another piece of metal. We ran a number of dives and approaches and they could pick us up from about 2,000 yards away. All it took was a click from our K-Bars. We did not have luck hearing the submarine, but we found that by swimming on the surface, waiting for the submarine approach, we could spot the sub's periscope breaking the surface with a consistent "feather wave" of phosphorescence as it approached through the salt water. As it approached at two knots, it would slow down and avoid broaching and we could then skin it to the foredeck of the submarine. We would arrange for a line to run from the forward top of the conning tower down to the foredeck, lashed just forward of where we entered the foredeck of the submarine. The escape tower side hatch would be left open and all we had to do was swim in, secure the hatch, blow the escape trunk, undo the torpedo room hatch, and climb down the ladder into the forward torpedo room. The sub's exec, who usually ran all escape trunk controls, could close his overhead hatch that formed the bottom of the escape trunk and then he would open sea flood, fill the trunk back and open the side hatch, ready for the next recon divers to enter.

Diving Physicals and Buoyant Ascents

BEFORE WE UNDERTOOK our one-week learning experiences at the submarine escape tower at Pearl Harbor, our diving medical officer (DMO) wanted each of us making the first buoyant ascents from a United States submarine to go through another dive physical. I was in full agreement, but I wanted to add another safety precaution. I asked our doc if he could arrange for another physician to "help out" with this special physical. I suggested that it would be a prudent idea to have a psychiatrist tapping our chest and taking our pulse and vital signs. He thought that was a good idea. We both opted to not tell our divers that the "tapping and listening" lieutenant was a shrink—a clinical psychologist. I felt that Captains DeFazio and McKinstry and I (a senior major at the time) had done the most critical evaluation of each of our divers to execute the first live buoyant ascents possible. The doc and I talked to the shrink with just the three of us there. I asked him to listen to us to see if any of our divers showed an indication or tendency of getting "clausty" (claustrophobic). He agreed and said that he would.

After the physicals, the doc and I talked to the shrink. His response was that he had listened to everything the divers had to say and there was absolutely no indication that any of our divers would get clausty. He told us that we had done reselection very well. That resolved any concerns that we had about our divers, and we were off to Pearl Harbor for a week of nothing but buoyant ascents and skinning it in at fifty feet. There was some concern in Commander Submarines from the CNO's office about the danger of air embolism that causes death in three seconds if anyone does not continuously exhale all spare air in a nine-second ascent. They were thus very pleased that we received certification from our DMO for buoyant ascent clearance.

Man-in-the-Sea Monument

LITTLE HAS BEEN WRITTEN about the yeoman work of our Marine Corps divers. That is beginning to change. Divers from all other services (USN, USA, USAF, and USCG) began to take great interest in our joint Marine Corps recon diver/ submarine crews and DMO's joint development of our exit and recovery techniques and operational use. After retirement, in about 2003, I was asked by HQMC to act as the Marine Corps representative on a Man-in-the-Sea project. I felt honored by my designation. I had been an "0-6 full colonel" for forty-five years, and the lead diver in much of the submarine diving development, and the first Navy diver to make a live buoyant operational ascent from any U.S. submarine. I had to presume that these were the reasons that HQMC, two commandants, and former JCS chairman Gen. Peter Pace collectively asked me to represent all of our Marine Corps divers.

When completed, this will be a monument dedicated to military divers from all services and government agencies. It will be a ten- to eleven-foot-tall bronze sculpture of a figure using the MKV diving helmet and suit. The nickname for the monument is "Jake." It is to be located on the Anacostia Riverwalk trail, fittingly near the former site of the Navy diving training school.

Unusual Request for Submarine Diving

OCCASIONALLY FORCE RECON COMPANY would get a request that was out of the ordinary. Warner Brothers Studio in Hollywood needed some help with a movie they were about to film, *Up Periscope,* using a USN submarine. Force Recon was on the list to be the next entity scheduled for submarine departure and return to the submarine. I took the call from a Marine lieutenant colonel who was the public affairs officer for both the First MarDiv (our parent command) and the Marine Corps base. He advised that he had heard from Warner Brothers that they were asking the Marine Corps for help on an upcoming movie entailing submarine diving and re-entry. It was to star actors James Garner and Edmond O'Brien. Marine Corps Headquarters had given their approval, if we could fit it into our schedule. I then received a telephone call from Howard Koch, who identified himself as the producer and director of the Garner movie.

He explained what he wanted the swimmer to do: this was the part James Garner was playing. I saw no problem with what they were asking of me, so he sent me a script with artist sketches of the shots that he wanted to get with Garner's character exiting the submerged submarine and swimming out and away from the sub, then later swimming back. In the movie, Edmond O'Brien, who played the skipper, was waiting patiently for Garner to complete his mission and return to the sub so that they could exit the lagoon on a Japanese-occupied island in the South Pacific. The next week I was asked to come to lunch in San Diego to meet their technical advisor, a retired submarine rear admiral. It went well, and he agreed with how I was to do the swimming. When this whole request started, it was my intention to let one of our young divers do the swimming required. At that time, all of my submarine-qualified divers were of fairly short height. They wanted someone who was six-feet-three-inches tall with a short haircut. I met both requirements, so they asked me to do the swimming. I agreed. James Garner was in good physical condition, and I was to wear his clothes as he and I were the same height, and he also had a short haircut. My hair had gone gray at my temples when I was a rifle company commander. They saw no problem with that and sprayed my hair a darker color to match Garner's hair.

Our submarine was to get underway from San Diego, and I would rendezvous at the location where the sub was going to flood down with about sixteen feet of water over the foredeck. She was not going to be underway, so it looked as if it would be an easy swim. We arrived in a Navy "camera barge," which was like a smaller version of a PT (patrol torpedo) boat. The chief petty officer who was going to do the photography was very experienced. He briefed me on the arm and hand signals that he would use to direct me when to exit the escape trunk and swim away, go out about fifty yards, turn around, and come back to the sub. I was to pull out my dive knife (I used my Ka-Bar) and bang on the hull and then enter the escape trunk. Simple and straightforward or, so we thought. In force recon, when we were diving on any mission from the submarine, I required a safety diver to accompany a diver on such a mission. That was going to be no problem, since the submarine was just partially submerged, so that the top of the conning tower was above and just out of the water. We were at a dead stop. The day was clear, and we had excellent visibility, so my safety diver was almost above the chief at his camera on the foredeck. He could see the escape trunk and my route out across the bow to swim Garner's mission.

ONE SLIGHT PROBLEM DEVELOPED that began to obscure an otherwise very straightforward swim. As my safety diver and I dropped off the rear of the PT boat-like camera barge, we both dipped our heads down to clear our dive masks. Two blue sharks, one slightly over six feet and the other about six feet, swam underneath us checking us out. We had about seventy-five yards to swim, the safety diver to the conning tower and me to join the chief (our main photographer) on the foredeck near the tripod underwater camera.

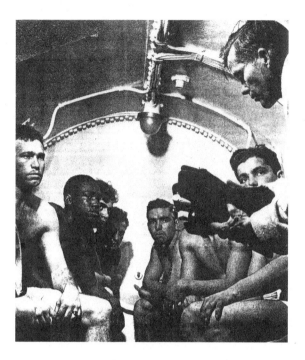

Decompression chamber, which was used by divers who rapidly ascended from the depths.

I looked over at my safety diver, and he was expressing alarm/dissatisfaction. He yelled, "Jesus Christ, Skipper. Did you see them? What are we going to do?"

To reassure him and restore whatever remaining confidence he had, I tried to be cool and reassuring. I told him that we both had bottles (SCUBA), and we were going to get below the surface about five feet and slowly swim to the sub, which was seventy-five yards away. I told him to swim back-to-back with me, he would go to the conning tower and I would go contact the chief, our photographer. I reminded the safety diver that if the sharks came toward us to face them, and if their nose was in front, to tap the shark on the nose. That is a very sensitive area, and our experience had been that when you do that, the sharks would swim away.

We carefully and slowly got to the sub. It was my perception that the two sharks were just curious and once we dropped below the surface and were on their level, that we were no longer a possible nibbling site. The swim camera shootings went well; I must have done the same route and return about nine or ten times. At that point I thought to myself, "Being a movie actor and having to do take after take is hard work, and actors don't have the cushy deal that many of us think they have." One final small incident: Garner was supposed to have cut himself on the pier in the

Sketch of the action sequence for "Up Periscope."

Japanese lagoon, and he had a plain white bandage wrapped around the spot. The cloth bandage came off on about take eight or nine and began to slowly sink to the bottom. This intrigued the sharks who were still curious (in my opinion), and they made for the water just below my legs where the fake bandage was making its way slowly to the bottom. They came to about six feet below my legs and then did the most gorgeous slow roll, which exposed their stomachs and their open mouths and a nice display of shark teeth. They ran their bodies past the descending fake bandage to check it out and then just kept on going.

Arm and hand signals from the photographer (Navy chief, diver) gave me a thumbs-up, indicating to me he felt we were through. The sub blew her ballast and surfaced fully. The chief, my safety diver, and I met to discuss the shoot. I left feeling that Warner Brothers was satisfied.

Two days later I got a call from Koch. He seemed pretty excited, so I listened. He asked if I realized that I had two pretty good-sized sharks swimming in and out of most of my takes. I responded that I had, but after swimming with them a little while, I felt that they were just curious. Koch then told me that it was too bad that he could not have left some of those sharks with me in the film they were going to use. He said there was not enough "lead in" and "lead out" to be able to keep the sharks in, so they ended up on Warner Brothers' cutting room floor.

ABOUT A MONTH LATER, Koch called me and invited Jo and me to Warner Brothers for lunch with Jim Garner and to the studio preview with Garner, O'Brien, and the others later that afternoon. It was very pleasant. Never having spent much time around movie actors, I took the opportunity to talk to Jim Garner about how he got into the movies. He was very relaxed, and we had a good conversation for about half an hour. He told me that he had researched where all of the directors and producers would gas their cars. Then, he got a job there, filling gas tanks and wiping windshields. He did this for about four months, hitting on them and asking for a chance at a screen test. He was then drafted into the Army. He came to Korea in about 1951 and was assigned to the infantry in the Seventh Division, which for a time was on the left flank of our First Marine Division. As former order of battle officer for the First MarDiv, I remembered their division call sign, which was "Bayonet."

Jim Garner was wounded twice in combat, and he was sent back to the U.S. and discharged. He got his old job back at the gas station in Hollywood. This time, they learned of his two wounds and gave him a screen test. He played in a war movie about WW II, went on to star as a cowboy in the "Maverick" TV series for Warner Brothers and then had an increasingly busy career as an actor. He signed a nice 8 x 10 photo for me, which is at my ocean house. It simply says, "Thanks for doing the stunt swimming for me on Up Periscope." I liked him before this whole event and after as well. He was one normal, solid guy.

Turning to Our Jumpers, Our Next Task Was to Locate a Usable, Carrier-Qualified Aircraft

OUR FIRST TASK with respect to developing a capability of jumping from and inserting Marine parachutists from carrier aircraft was finding a carrier-qualified aircraft that we could work with. We had to develop off-carrier capabilities. I first went to our Marine aviators at El Toro and confirmed what my earlier research revealed: After World War II, the Marine Corps had only the Douglas F3D2 night fighter that was carrier-qualified. The Marine aviators suggested that we talk to the Navy at North Island, NAS in Coronado, CA. In May 1956. My parachute platoon leader Capt. Taylor, Sgt. Zwiener (our parachute rigger and packer) and I started more detailed research with naval air at North Island, NAS. We finally got to Fleet Logistic Wing, Pacific. They ran all carrier-on-board delivery (COD) aircraft. They owned and ran COD flights and schedules all over the Pacific. Their aircraft was the

Author (left) and actor James Garner during a break in Garner's hit TV show, "Maverick."

Grumman TF-1. At the squadron, Lt. Cdr. Roy Taylor (no relation to my exec. Joe Taylor) was one of their lead pilots.

The TF-1 was a twin-engine, high wing transport that carried up to nine jumpers. It had two very powerful engines – the Wright R-1820-82,1525 horsepower each. We found the TF-1 easily adaptable for jumping static line parachuting; static line requires a secure cable of good strength. Fortunately, the TF-1 had two 13-foot "I" beams mounted fore and aft on the overhead of the aircraft. These were used for transport of atomic weapons to aircraft carriers. The only rigging to prepare the aircraft for jumping was the nut-and-bolt attachment of our jump cable (one-quarter inch steel), which ran just an inch below and along the thirteen-foot I-beams.

The only problem was that Grumman Aircraft had never contemplated their aircraft being used as a jump platform for parachutists. We worked on this with the Navy's parachute center at El Centro on the Mexican border.

The exit door was divided in half (vertically). The forward part of the left entry door was used for people entering and leaving the aircraft on the ground. The aft (rear) half of the door was used to load atomic weapons, by hooking them up to the thirteen-foot rails.

Because the Grumman TF-1 had never been jumped, we became experimental parachutists and worked closely with the test parachute engineers on the staff at El

Centro. Grumman advised that the TF-1 had never been flown with both halves of the side door removed. I had our pilot, Lt. Cdr. Roy Taylor examine the door frames in question on both doors. His evaluation that it was built like a brick outhouse was fully agreed upon by the Grumman designers, engineers, and construction people who put the airplane together. There was some initial concern about flutter or vibration when flying without both doors. In that the aluminum edge of the door frame was fairly sharp, as a precaution we padded and taped the door as part of the prep of the TF-1 for live jumping of parachutists.

We were very careful in all of our evaluations. We used two, two-hundred-pound articulated dummies, rigged with T-10 static-line parachutes, with T7A Reserves. Using air-to-air photography, dropping at a hundred knots (later at one hundred twenty knots) with one-third flaps, we viewed the air-to-air photography with El Centro's parachute engineers and all of their qualified test parachutists. All hands agreed that everything appeared safe, so we were "good to go."

On the first live tests of the TF-1 to evaluate it for parachute exit, I jumped number one; CWO Vinson, senior test parachutist of the Navy was number two; Capt. Larry Neipling, USA, (from Fort. Benning Airborne) jumped number three; and a fourth test parachutist was from Naval Parachute Test Center. We jumped using both air-to-air and ground-to-air photography, and again found no major problems. The exit, with both doors removed, was just a bit tight (height was only forty-nine inches) dictating a somewhat-crouched exit stance. Of more concern, Marine parachutists emphasize a forceful, powerful exit jumping into the slipstream. The left engine nacelle was only sixty-seven inches from the jump door. The nacelle extended twenty-three inches to the rear of the door. We were concerned that our jumpers making a positive and forceful exit would leap out and strike the engine nacelle. The 1,525 horsepower engine was only eight feet forward of the door. A three-bladed prop forcing that much slipstream air through that narrow space immediately turned the jumper's body ninety degrees to the left to a facing-the-tail direction. We quickly determined that despite the most forceful exit we could execute, the venturi effect on the jumper's body was so great that it turned the TF-1 into an ideal jumpers' airplane. Our anticipated short space/clearance of the engine nacelle problem was solved. We jumped it day and night under all variations of airspeed and flap settings over the next five days. At the end of the week, we now had a "parachute, carrier-qualified aircraft, good to operate anywhere in the world." We celebrated our festivities that night with an adult libation. On July 26, 1956, we made the first off-carrier operational parachute jump in naval aviation history. Using Commander Taylor as our pilot from VR-5, we took off from North Island with four jumpers for recovery

First jump from Grumman TF-1.
Author is in the air below the exit hatch and Force Recon sergeant-major is "in the door."

eighty miles at sea aboard USS *Bennington* (CVA-20) and recovered aboard. My boss, Col. Fuller, XO of Marine Corps Test Unit One, was not going to sit this one out. He came on board with us as an official observer, and flew with us on the jump, which we did into Naval Parachute Test Center, El Centro. We landed in the desert.

Jumpers were me, my officers, and enlisted: Capt. Don Koelper (later KIA in Saigon, his was the first Navy Cross awarded by the Marine Corps in Vietnam), and PFCs Ken R. Ball and Mathew J. O'Neill Jr. (he was later killed in one of our operational jumps at Camp Pendleton at Case Springs).

The next month, August 1956, we began operationally jumping our first jet fighters for insertion of Marine parachutists—the Marine Corps F3D2. We jumped with one parachutist to each aircraft. We would ride in the right seat of the aircraft, the pilot in the left seat. On oxygen initially up to drop altitude, we would come off oxygen, carefully get up, step over the console between the pilot and radar operator, turn 180 degrees, and get into the chute behind both pilot seats. This chute reminded me of my days in Seattle as a youth, sliding down my grandmother's coal chute used to supply coal for their home.

Extending our bodies down the chute with our jump boots just showing, we waited at the bottom of the chute. We hung on to a small monkey bar and looked back at the pilot toward the front of the aircraft. Our first jumps were ground controlled. The drop-zone commander would advise the pilot to drop as he flew over our DZ thousands of feet below. The pilot merely reached back and tapped us on our helmets. We let go, and we would slide down the chute in a free-fall delay until reaching opening altitude. At first, we would only take five- to ten-second delays. Later as we became more comfortable jumping from jets, Sgt. Zwiener and I dropped in formation from twenty-five thousand feet over Camp Pendleton; we both opened at seventy seconds at about two thousand feet. No problems.

...

Parachutist exiting between the jet's two engines, going "down the slide" from the cockpit. 1957.

When we started operationally jumping jets (F3D2, A3D, AJ1), someone started an urban myth. The myth was, "If you jump from jets, it will affect your sexual performance." Hearing this, I contacted a flight surgeon friend. He advised that he had looked into this allegation on behalf of the many pilots who may have to exit a jet.

I told the flight surgeon that I had jumped from Navy/Marine jet aircraft twenty-one times. My recon jumpers during this same time frame had stacked up more than four hundred jet jumps, east and west coast combined. In none of these four hundred and twenty-one jumps had any parachutist noticed any effect on their sexual habits, that is, difficulty in erection.

Marines are not conversationally talkative about their sexual habits, but as a result of my being around Marines for a number of years, particularly parachutists, the shooting-the-breeze conversations would occasionally touch on sexual activities. In all of those times, I had yet to hear any Marine complain about inability to perform.

When jumping jets, each of us usually wore a protective jock strap. I never heard a complaint, or any questions asked that jumping from a jet caused any problems. I concluded on my own that there was no apparent evidence that jet jumping causes any negative aspect of such parachuting. Discussing it openly put the urban myth to rest.

CHAPTER 16

Okinawa and Triple Canopy Ops
1959-1960

I n January 1959, I had turned over command of First Force Recon (FMF) Company
to my then-exec. I had formed and led First Force for its first twenty months in the
Fleet Marine Force (in 2014 they celebrated fifty-seven years of force recon service to
the Marine Corps). Although I had been in the FMF since its formation, it was time
for me to return to an infantry unit. Lt. Col. Bill Chipp had just left the First Mar
Div Reconnaissance Battalion, and he asked if I would like to be his S-3 (operations
officer). Bill and I had gotten to know each other over the previous two years and
we were comfortable with each of our operational styles of working with troops. The
exec was Maj. John Bushrod Wilson. We had a good staff, and I was looking forward
to a thirteen-month deployment from Camp Pendleton to Okinawa, or on "the
Rock" (recon Marines' nickname for Okinawa).

We became the first "transplacement battalion" in the Marine Corps. The
concept was sound. We would form Marine infantry battalions and one-half of the
complement would be assigned to that one battalion for twenty-four months. One-
half of the battalion would be assigned for one year. That way, the transplacement
battalion would train together and stay together for two years for half and one year
for the remainder. We were First Battalion, First Marine Regiment (1/1) as part of
the First Marine Division at Camp Pendleton. When we arrived on Okinawa our

name designation changed to 1/9 (First Battalion, Ninth Marine Regiment), part of the presently deployed Ninth Marines, part of the Third Marine Division.

Final predeployment training went well, and we embarked for the Rock on schedule. Upon arrival, we quickly took over the former barracks of 1/9. It was being disbanded as we arrived. Our barracks were in Sukiran on mid-southern Okinawa, slightly to the south and east of Kadena AFB. Being the first transplacement battalion in operations, one could see the detailed planning that had preceded us. We were set-up on a well-designed training schedule, and when it came time for our annual rifle qualification firing, all of the necessary ranges had been prearranged. This is not to say that we were slavishly following some prior G-3's master plan. It just meant that we had the advantage of having an efficient and coordinated plan.

We had the usual deployments that every FMF infantry battalion goes through. Cold weather training had been set up on mainland Japan (Honshu), where we lived in tents in the snow on the slopes of Mount Fuji. We did a landing in the Philippines and had the chance to get into Manila on liberty instead of the usual place, Olongapo. While in the Philippines, we did some jungle training in Subic Bay.

We spent a month off-island in British North Borneo on the first joint South East Asia Treaty Organization (SEATO) landing. Two units from the British Army joined us for the jungle operations in the Sarawak area. This was the former jungle area of the Dyaks and Iban tribes, who were headhunters. The units from the British Army taught us a lot about operations in triple canopy jungle (all of which paid off in later deployments to Vietnam). We operated first with the Seventeenth Gurkhas and then with the "First Sherwood Foresters," (obviously from Notts and Darby in England), a source for many Robin Hood jokes. Both units came from their jungle station in Malaya. It was a great experience operating with them. Because of insurgency threats in other parts of Southeast Asia, our battalion on Okinawa trained for and did several "air mount-out" standbys waiting on the runway in C-130s to take us to the sound of guns. We did make a helicopter-borne landing from the decks of the USS *Princeton*, with our landing in the Gau Shan Mountains in Taiwan. We were surprised to have a visit there from President Chiang Kai-shek, complete with hamburg hat and Prince Albert coat.

I LEFT 1/1 at the end of our thirteen-month deployment with orders to go to HQMC, Washington, DC. We collectively came away with the same impression, that for operational readiness the adoption of the transplacement battalion concept was a good decision by the Marine Corps.

As a result of some close relationships that we had with the British and Gurkha officers who came over from Malaya to Okinawa and took part in the planning for Operation Saddle Up, I was later invited by the British to "come on over to Malaya and do some jungle patrols with us." I look on that invitation, and my later patrols with British forces, to be some of the highlights of our deployment.

Back in 1959 (long before we had computers or e-mail), we had to resort to writing letters, or, in the military we could send a dispatch, which was like a telegram. My battalion commander in 1/9, Col. Chip of our transplacement battalion on Okinawa, agreed with me that the invitation from the British would be a great opportunity to learn current jungle operations. Our Third Marine Division commander felt the same. It became obvious that I would have to get permission from the commandant of the Marine Corps.

I decided to send a dispatch to the commandant, Gen. David M. Shoup. In 1959, I requested permission to take thirty days leave to go to Malaya to patrol with the Brits. He granted it with stipulation that I brief his headquarters staff and other Marine units on my lessons learned. There was no money involved, and I had to pay my own way to Malaya from Okinawa.

Deep jungle patrol in northern Malaya during the British/Malaysian campaign against the Communists, July 1959.

The Malaya Experience in Triple Canopy Jungle

I HITCHED A RIDE on a Marine aircraft to Hong Kong. I paid my own fare on Air India to Bangkok ($80) and then paid for a ticket on a small narrow-gage railway to the Malayan border ($26). It was a pretty primitive train to say the least. There were no glass windows, or any kind of windows, and one sat on plain wooden benches for the trip. The local Thai children were delightful to watch as the small train rattled its way down the Thai portion of the Malay Peninsula toward the southern Thai border. The children would hang out from the sides of the passenger cars and sing and talk vociferously.

At the border I was met by the Gurkhas and Brits who were in one of their British Army Land Rovers. I was with them for three weeks. While in Malaya, the RAF flew me places in their jungle transport, a "Pioneer" twin-tail, a bit like our Marine Corps Flying Boxcar, the R4D (Fairchild C-119). From the Thai border, they drove me to Taiping, a small tin-mining town in northern Malaya. Here, I was taken under the wing of Lt. Col. Kim Morrison of the New Zealand Army. He was highly decorated, and, in order to get command, he had had to drop down one rank from being a "proper" colonel to becoming a lieutenant colonel. For this assignment, he was commanding the First New Zealand infantry battalion. Under his command, I was issued a full kit of two sets of British jungle utilities, and two pairs of British Malayan jungle boots.

They had me wearing a British major's crown insignia so that I would not appear to be an American Marine. I was issued a 9mm, a Sterling Patchett. My patrol was operating out of a rubber plantation outside of the very small Malayan village of Liman Kati. I was fortunate to participate in each of the three major types of patrols that British forces were using: ambush patrols, curfew patrols through the rubber estates at the end of the day to ensure all Malays went into the "relocation camps" to prevent the citizens from being approached and pressured for money or rice by the Communist terrorists (CTs), and a deep-jungle patrol in triple canopy. Our patrols slept in tents, which were very similar to our Marine Corps squad tents, while encamped on the edge of the Michelin rubber plantation near Liman Kati. There were about eight cots to each tent. While on the deep-jungle patrol, we slept in nylon hammocks, strung between two trees. We had a portion of a cut-up nylon cargo chute so that we could cover our faces while sleeping through the night to prevent bugs and leeches from attaching to our faces.

The troops in our platoon that patrolled together kept a small, furry dog as a pet while in camp. It was friendly and made friends with all our troop. One day the pup went missing. We looked everywhere. Our squad tents were mounted on wooden floors that were about two feet above the irregular jungle floor. Sure enough, we there found a six-foot python about six inches in diameter, digesting a large lump just aft of its mouth. All of us were convinced that the python had eaten our puppy. Everyone agreed to try to get the puppy out of the python. Two troopers held the python while a fighting knife was used to cut open the python's belly, in essence a "puppyectomy." Not knowing how long it had been since it had been ingested, someone tried mouth-to-mouth resuscitation, but the puppy had expired in the belly of the unlucky python. At this point, all of us involved decided to go to the local charwallah, a small Chinese concessionaire typically found around small towns and rubber plantations and tin mines, for a cold beer (to drown the loss of our small dog). When my Marine peers heard that I was taking a thirty-day leave, they berated me and told me that I was bereft of sense to go to Malaya for these patrols.

• • •

Jo was not happy, but she also was aware that I could not have come home on such a leave. She later became quite aware of how much that period of time gave to me professionally. Jo had concurred with my patrols but was particularly happy years later when I took her to Malaya with several British friends. We rode the brand new Eastern Orient Express on its second run since being put in service, from Bangkok to Singapore. This was a three-day ride down the Malay Peninsula with stops in Penang, the capital, and in Kuala Lumpur. It was a bit pricey but well worth it. On this later trip to Malaya while retired from the Marine Corps, working as a law school associate dean and associate professor, one dressed for dinner in full kit, that is, formal wear (tuxes or dinner jackets) and miniatures. I could not help but think of the Raj and Rudyard Kipling.

The train, when running through the rubber plantations, had to go slowly because of the lack of a stable-base railroad bed for the train tracks. My wife thus gained an appreciation for our curfew patrols during my operations in June 1959.

Singapore

TIME PASSED QUICKLY, and I was sent down-country, eventually arriving in Singapore. I was given officer quarters at the famous Changi barracks in Singapore. This was the site of Changi prison that housed some six thousand Brits and other nationalities during World War II after the fall of Singapore. While there, I made friends with an Australian pilot, and he got me on an RAF flight to Hong Kong at no cost. From Hong Kong, I was able to get on a Marine R&R (rest and relaxation) flight back to Okinawa.

This was in 1959. During the "emergency," as the British describe it, the CTs had an in-jungle troop strength in excess of eleven thousand. By 1959, the CTs had been reduced to just under eight hundred As they neared the end of the emergency, the CTs were using the Thai border in northern Malaya as a refuge. They would patrol briefly and then slip north across the border into southern Thailand. The Thais would cooperate with the British forces, and they began to cut off that sanctuary. The British in Malaya had a number of fine officers who brought several different approaches to the campaign.

Most agreed that Gen. Gerald Templer[1] was by far the most successful. Under his leadership, tactics were closely evaluated. The majority of major kills were from carefully set ambushes. Many of the other kills were from rather random encounters, such as while on curfew patrol, usually through the many rubber estates. While evaluating the many reports of contact, the British commanders discovered that the average length of contact in the jungle was usually less than one minute. Special training of troops for deep jungle patrols paid off many times over. The British called upon natives from several of their other British jungle territories. The battalion (1/9) that I was operating with as the S-3 operations officer was in British North Borneo on the Brunei Peninsula, operating in the Sarawak area, inland from the coast. In this area were the two major tribes of the headhunters: the Ibans and the Dyaks. Both successfully accompanied British and Gurkha patrols, not so much with Malayan police or Malayan Army patrols. They were used as instructors, and our Iban tracker was most helpful when I was doing last minute preparations for our deep jungle patrol. These natives gave us tips on leeches, where to get water when not near a jungle stream (cut a nearby water vine and drink it directly), and similar information.

The Dyaks were used for patrol for a time by the British, but greater success was experienced when using the Iban. The Iban are born in the jungle and are considered by the locals to be "mountain people."

On deep jungle patrols, we crossed streams five to six times a day, which was much more frequently than I had experienced in the Marine Corps. Thus, there was not much point in trying to avoid streams. You relied upon the mesh drain holes in your issue jungle boots to let the water out, and the heat and the constant movement dried out the jungle boots pretty quickly. The New Zealand infantry battalion (a bit smaller in size than our normal Marine battalion) showed me how to use patrol dogs.[2]

Back on Okinawa after the Malaya experience, I was a "deployed bachelor" with

---

1 Field Marshal Sir Gerald Walter Robert Templer, KG, GCB, GCMG, KBE, DSO, fought in both World Wars. He is best know for his defeat of the guerrilla rebels in Malaya. He died in 1979.
2 See Chapter 25, "Lessons Learned," about our use of patrol dogs in Vietnam.

my wife and three sons back in Seattle. I decided to use my evenings alone to write an article about my jungle experiences. Never having written a magazine article before, I wrote "Malaya Jungle Patrols." The *Marine Corps Gazette* bought my article and put it in their professional magazine that was just beginning a series on counter insurgency.

I was paid over a thousand dollars for that article and its pictures. Our thirteen-month deployment came to an end. I had requested duty in Washington, D.C., and my request was granted.

I THEN RETURNED TO DUTY at HQMC. I was asked by the commandant to brief him and his staff on my patrols with the Brits. I dressed in the full British kit and uniform. I even borrowed a Sten gun (unloaded) from our Marine armory in Quantico. I then marched in to the tune of "The Bridge on the River Kwai." During my briefing, I was asked by Gen. Shoup how I felt our Marine equipment stood up in the jungle and triple canopy. I told him frankly that our boondockers (boots) disintegrated within seven days. I told him about the boots that the British had developed, made of green cotton fabric, with rubber-cleated soles with drain holes to permit drying after going through jungle streams. Sensing his interest in these boots, I gave him the spare pair of the two pairs that I had been issued. I still have the others.

Gen. Shoup, who was seated next to his quartermaster (QM) general (whose name I do not remember), gave him my spare pair and asked me what I would suggest. I advised them to send my spare British jungle boots up to the Army Development Lab at Natick, Massachusetts. I suggested that they could "reverse engineer" the Brit boots and make a new type of jungle boot for our forces. That is exactly what they did, and the jungle boots that we used in Vietnam were designed from those jungle boots that I gave to the commandant.

• • •

Natick Labs improved upon the British boot and added working mesh that prevented leeches from getting into the boots. They made the boots out of light tan or green nylon fabric instead of the British cotton. Nylon dries more quickly. Lastly, they improved on the Brit boots by making a steel shank that ran the length of the boot and deflected punji stakes if one stepped on enemy punji stakes. Punji sticks are sharpened wooden stakes used by the CTs as a cheap, unsophisticated weapon. The sticks could be made by any villager with a sharp knife. All they did was sharpen them and then dip and treat them with urine (human or animal). When stepped upon, the sticks usually penetrated the foot, and they proved to infect almost immediately. Punji stakes were placed and hidden along jungle trails for the unwary to become incapacitated within a short time of being stepped upon.

Our military and the British have kept records and for anyone wounded and unable to move on their own, it takes an average of four persons to care for the wounded and get them to treatment. Thus punji stakes became a "force multiplier" for the CTs and had the effect of diminishing the number of British or Gurkha troops able to carry the fight to the Communist insurgents.

CHAPTER 17

White House Aide-de-Camp
1960-1961

Returning home from deployment was always exciting to get back with my family. We spent some time in Seattle visiting friends. Since my return was during summer vacation, we had no problem arranging for school records for our boys to transfer to school in Washington, D.C. We loaded up for our cross-country trip, and we were off to live in D.C.

Arriving in Washington, D.C. for extended duty at HQMC in G-3 operations, I was unaware of the protocol, or even that I was being considered for a special position. I was called by the commandant's chief of staff and advised that I was being reassigned to the White House as an aide-de-camp. I was a fairly senior major at the time. Apparently I had already been vetted by the U.S. Secret Service and had passed muster.

Outgoing President Dwight D. Eisenhower and his wife, Mamie, had left their residence at the White House by this time and were just waiting to go through all of the inaugural balls and get on with their retirement.

The chief of staff briefed all the aides. I was told that President John F. Kennedy had personally requested me because I was a Marine who reminded him of his interactions with Marines in the Solomon Islands. His PT-109 recovered some trapped Marines who were about to be taken by Japanese patrols. President Kennedy had asked me to escort Poet Laureate Robert Frost to all the inaugural events.

Several memorable events occurred while I was assigned as an aide at the White House. Most involved Poet Laureate Robert Frost. President Kennedy was quite specific in my orders: "You take care of Robert Frost. Stick with him, and make sure his needs are taken care of." With that guidance, I was given a Navy sedan and driver. I was prepared to escort Mr. Frost to each of the inaugural events he was set to attend.

He was a house guest in Georgetown at the home of Adlai Stevenson's sister. After I picked him up, he began asking me questions about my Marine Corps duties, my education, and so forth. After about ten minutes of conversation, Mr. Frost turned to me and asked, "You seem to have a pretty good education and good experiences. Why are you staying in the Marine Corps?" His tone imparted either a lack of understanding of the military or a put-down that being in the military was a less than desirable endeavor. I was immediately irritated by what Mr. Frost had asked or had implied by his comment and question. I suppressed my anger and finally composed an answer. I finally turned to him and formally addressed him, "Mr. Frost, I do what I do (being a Marine officer) so that you can do what you do (write poetry)." He didn't say anything for a moment and then turned to me and in an apologetic way said, "Bruce, you are right. You do indeed do what you do in order that I can do what I do." That ended the conversation on that subject, and, from that point on, we became good friends. It was "Bruce" and "Robert" from that point foreword.

The next day I was to pick up Robert and drive him to a poetry reading scheduled at the Library of Congress. The weather in Washington that week had been horrible. We had six inches of snow on the roads, and traffic was jammed. We were about ten minutes late getting to Georgetown. I rang the bell and there was no answer or sounds from inside the house.

I sent my driver to the closest gas station with the unlisted number. I could hear it ringing and no answer. I visualized the eighty-year-old Mr. Frost, having had a heart attack or fallen, scrabbling on the floor to reach the phone. I was already seeing the headlines: "Marine loses Poet Laureate of the West."

I was in Marine dress blues, and I climbed on top of the six-foot brick wall surrounding the Stevenson house. I made my way over a garage roof and found an unlocked window. I slid it open, went in, and swept the house, looking for his body. I was not thinking of my breaking and entering at that moment. He had panicked and gotten a cab and gone to the Library of Congress on his own. We finally surmised this and drove to the Library of Congress and met him there.

He later found out about my unusual entry, looking for him. On a photo of himself, he inscribed it: "To Bruce Meyers, My Friend and Protector. Robert Frost". I treasure that photo and look at it to this day. In reflecting back, I have been a number of places in my dress blues, but, have never "broken and entered" before or since.

During President Kennedy's inauguration on the east Capitol steps, our seats looked across at the Supreme Court building. The street was filled with more than ten thousand people to view the swearing-in ceremony. They had set up a podium, and President and Mrs. Eisenhower were seated next to the podium. President-elect Kennedy and his wife Jackie were seated next to them. Then, there was the full Supreme Court, the Joint Chiefs of Staff—in essence, the leadership of the free world was sitting within twenty feet of that podium.

Robert Frost was to read a special poem that he had written for his friend and soon-to-be president. I escorted Robert down the steps, between the Eisenhowers and the Kennedys, past the Supreme Court and the Joint Chiefs of Staff, to the podium. I helped Mr. Frost place the typewritten pages containing his poem on the podium. Suddenly, the podium began to smoke as if it was on fire.

Secret Service swarmed the smoking podium, thinking it might have been a bomb. They quickly determined it was just an electrical short in the mechanical device that made the podium go up and down, to accommodate different heights of speakers. Robert had not bound his poetry in any manner. It was a cold, windy January day. Pages of his poetry began to blow in the wind and out over the crowd. I just shook my head and placed my head in my hands. Robert Frost stepped up and recited

U.S. Capitol, January 21, 1961. Inauguration of John F. Kennedy.
Photo courtesy Architect of the Capitol..

his poem from memory. It went off without a hitch. We later found out that he had forgotten the poem that he wrote especially for Kennedy's inauguration, so he recited another poem. I had a copy of the actual newly written poem, and when I watched him reciting the poem at the inauguration, I knew that he had panicked and substituted another poem when his pages blew away. Everyone was pleased, and they did not know until later of his substitution.

To complete this story, the Kennedy family with just Robert Frost and me as his escort, went to the top of the Capitol building to a room that I did not know even existed. There was a small buffet arranged in this very small room at the very top of the Capitol. This was during a short period of time before the President's party was to embark in the presidential limousines for the ride down Pennsylvania Avenue to the White House to view the Inaugural Parade.

Robert Frost and I were standing together by ourselves. President Kennedy came over to us with a twinkle in his eye. He was very charismatic, and he expressed concern for Mr. Frost, saying something like, "I was worried, Robert, when I saw your poetry blow away." Both Robert Frost and I straightened up and came to attention. Robert Frost told President Kennedy, "After all, Mr. President, I wrote it." We both extended our hands to shake hands with President "Jack" Kennedy, "Congratulations, Mr. President." At that moment, he had been President for maybe fifteen minutes. I noted that this was the first time that both Robert Frost and I automatically used his new title, Mr. President. Before it was always "Jack" and "Robert" between the president and the poet. It was like some form of magic. When the President took the oath, their prior relationship was changed forever.

• • •

My father had also just finished law school, when as a young Army officer, he received a call from "his" White House. He was asked to become President Teddy Roosevelt's personal events secretary. When I was growing up he used to tell us about being at the White House. Before attending law school, he had enlisted in the Army for the Spanish American War in 1898. He graduated from George Washington Law in 1906. I don't know if my father had any contact with President Roosevelt prior to his assignment as social event secretary.

CHAPTER 18

The Pentagon Assignment
1961-1964

With respect to my temporary duty at the White House, I felt it should remain just that: temporary duty. I arranged to talk to our commandant, Gen. David M. Shoup, and I explained that I was married, had three sons, and a wife in Alexandria, Virginia. I explained that in my professional opinion, continuing such duty would be best by an unmarried person. He agreed, and after we completed reports on our White House duties, I was reassigned to the Secretary of Defense's office in the Pentagon in legislative affairs. My title was Deputy to the Assistant Secretary of Defense in Legislative Affairs. Everyone in this office was a lawyer but me. I had just my first year of law school completed.

Air Force Maj. Gen. Roderick became my boss. He agreed that probably the personnel assigners at HQMC had misread my BA in law as a law degree. I told Gen. Roderick that I wanted to finish law school and that I had been accepted at the George Washington University Law School. He was very supportive and kept my lack of a law degree from Marine Corps knowledge.

For the next three years, I worked in the "E-ring" (the term for the outer ring of the Pentagon with the largest offices and the best views of the Potomac and Washington across the Potomac River). Secretary of Defense Robert McNamara's offices were just seventy-five feet down the hall in the Pentagon's five-sided building, one of the largest buildings in Washington, other than the Capitol building. The offices were all on the inner rings going toward the open space courtyard, in the center of the pentagon-shaped building.

Lesser officers on the Pentagon pecking order were in offices toward the center courtyard. The assistant secretaries would be on the B-ring (the second ring), next the C-ring and so on down to the very center ring, a grass courtyard. Vehicles were kept to monstrous-sized parking lots, all arranged by order of rank and importance. Everyone walked in except the very senior civilian and military officials who would be dropped off at the entry steps on the E-ring or down in the drive-through garage in the basement of the Pentagon. There were various kinds of shops including a drug store, cleaners, and a small restaurant.

In that we were Secretary McNamara's legislative series of aides, with our office in legislative affairs, we responded to all congressional inquiries from both the House and Senate. Our cases would come to us with usually a short cover letter providing guidance from the congressman or senator or their staff regarding what they wanted to get back from the SecDef on the matter inquired about in the letter. Each of us had highly qualified and intelligent secretaries and administrative assistants who knew their way around and could help us on occasion with tips or guidance. The nine to ten officers and few civilians in our office were all lawyers. Initially, I was the only non-lawyer, but I was in the midst of finishing my last two years of George Washington Law School at night. Each of us handled certain subjects that were divided according to our specialties. One attorney handled all contractor inquiries, while others handled logistics, civil defense, installations, and other specialized areas. My area was manpower, which included all pay, personnel inquiries, service medicine, women in the armed forces, chaplains and religious matters, and all other "people matters." The system worked well and ran smoothly.

Embarrassing Moment

I HAD TO ACCOMPANY Department of Defense (DoD) witnesses and attend many congressional and committee meetings. From this, I will share my most embarrassing moment of my lifetime. I was late and running for a committee meeting. I was in uniform, greens and ribbons. As I raced around a corner, I ran right into a gorgeous woman and knocked her to the marble floor. I landed between her legs, right on top of her. The lady was Ted Kennedy's wife, Joan Bennett Kennedy. She had been running as well. She was very poised and cool, and she asked me in a delightfully low voice if I didn't think "it would be a good idea" for me to get us up and both depart the area. We did, to the delight of four capital police, all of whom I knew and three of whom were night law students with me at George Washington Law School.

Neither Mrs. Kennedy nor I was injured, but both of us were terribly embarrassed. Thank God there were no cameras so usually prevalent on the Hill.

After that close encounter, I always felt a bit sorry for her, especially after she and the senator divorced. My law school classmates never let me forget that moment.

THE TIME WENT QUICKLY. The boys were in great schools and did well. I was able to finish law school in the summer of 1963, and I learned a lot on the hill from some very intelligent people. I had orders as a lieutenant colonel (almost two years) as I entered senior school at Quantico. As I left the DOD, I was pleased to receive the first Joint Service Commendation Medal ever awarded. Since it was the first ever given for service on a joint staff, no one at Quantico knew what it was when I reported in. I received an artist's certificate of the award, since they had not even printed them yet. It was signed to me personally by Secretary McNamara.

My last three weeks of law school had me commuting to Quantico to attend Senior School during the day and coming back to Washington for evening classes. I finally graduated in the summer of 1963, with honors and the Order of the Coif, and elected to the law review. I owe each of my boys and Jo a great deal for their tremendous support that enabled me to finish law school and my tour as the deputy to Secretary of Defense.

I am appreciative of the duty, the friends and colleagues I met and got to know, and also for the opportunity to complete my law degree. A number of my colleagues helped along the way. Thank you.

Letter from President Kennedy

SEVERAL MONTHS AFTER LEAVING DUTY at the White House, I had pretty well integrated into the group of eleven attorneys—I was now about half way to graduation from George Washington Law School. We frequently had meetings where everyone not involved in hearings or other absences would gather to keep everyone current on our respective activities in the event another attorney might have to step in to help on one of our cases.

This meeting my secretary came in unannounced, and she was holding a letter by the tips of her fingers as if it contained deadly news! I immediately asked what her problem was. She replied it was a letter for me. I was surprised that she would interrupt a meeting and because she was my secretary, I knew she was highly qualified and that she always opened all of my mail.

The meeting became quickly silent when she advised that this was a letter from President Kennedy addressed to me. On opening and reading the document, I realized it was from the President's personal notepad. The President had a question for me about my article in the *Marine Corps Gazette* article published under the title "Malaya Jungle Patrols."

President Kennedy's questions to me were simple and straight forward: "What the hell were you doing in Malaya, in a war that we (the United States) were not involved in, and fighting alongside Gurkhas and British against the Communist terrorists?"

I immediately called my editor at the *Gazette* and asked his advice. He advised me to respond to the President immediately and be truthful, rapid, and accurate in my response. I did and responded, "I had made friends with the Gurkha and British officers, then serving in Malaya against the CT," and that they invited me to "come down and patrol with us in the triple canopy." I also told the President that I had learned much from my experience and that our Commandant had asked me to brief his staff at Headquarters Marine Corps, which I had done.

CHAPTER 19

The Senior School, Quantico, Virginia
1964-1965

The Marine Corps is generally considered to have four levels of instruction for its career officers. The Basic School (TBS) includes new second lieutenants from each of the service academies. I have had officers from Annapolis, West Point, the Air Force Academy, and graduates of every NROTC unit and university in the country work for me when I was XO and then CO the next year at TBS. The duration of TBS varied, over the years, but generally it ran six months to almost a year. The curriculum is rigid and great emphasis is placed on physical conditioning and fitness.

Next is our middle-level school. It is called the Junior School and is scoped for senior first lieutenants and captains who are company level-commanders (for example, rifle company commanders, battalion staff officers, and other assignments including assistant G-3, the S-2 Intelligence officer, the S-4 logistics officer).

Our third level of officer education includes the Senior School, the highest in-house educational program within the Corps, with tactics and leadership scoped toward the battalion commanders and staffs of similar units. It is predominantly for senior majors or lieutenant colonels. Maj. universities such as George Washington University have graduate-level programs for those who have not yet obtained a master's degree. The faculty is a group of resident professors at the Senior School. There is strong pressure on all career officers to have master's degrees by the time they graduate from the Senior School. Considerable emphasis is placed on the writing and publishing of researched papers. The Grey Research Library is on campus and is used by all. Many of the articles written are submitted to the *Marine Corps Gazette* and the research library publishes many of them.

The highest level of professional education is at the War College level. The National War College has students from each of the armed forces. Each of the other major services has a war college: the Army War College; the Navy War College, senior course; the Air University; and the Industrial College, administered by the Army War College. These are graduate-accredited universities, and virtually every graduate of these institutions will earn a master's degree from a host of disciplines. Selection is done by panels of generals and senior officers who review all potential students and select for attendance at one of the war colleges. During summer months, resident two-week courses are held at the Senior School mostly for Marine Reserve officers. Two of our Senior School classmates graduated, but were held over to be instructors for the summer. In my class, the two graduates held back as the Senior School instructors were Lt. Col. Angus McDonald and me. We were told to look on this delay joining one of the Marine divisions late as "an honor." Neither my friend Angus nor I considered it so. We would be coming in late to our division and missing key commands that were turning over, cutting us out of any chance for early command assignment. It also made us late for assignment of housing, and our kids were sometimes delayed in their schooling.

Another way of looking at this system of holding back—it also gave some of us the midyear chance for key commands. For me, it gave me the assignment as battalion commander of the landing force of the Sixth Fleet (commonly referred to as the "Med Battalion"). I believe the statistics are that only two of nine lieutenant colonels become eligible for this sought-after assignment each year.

I did well in the Senior School and ended up in the top ten of my class. My year-end research had been done on the varying of landing craft to support different missions during amphibious landings. It was well received and was selected by Commandant Shoup for special publication. I completed the summer as a "Senior School instructor" primarily for the many senior reserve officers that come to Quantico to improve their professional education. Summer went by quickly and was not as onerous as I had been led to expect. We were quickly en route to Camp Lejeune, and I was towing my nineteen-foot Lightning sailboat that we had acquired in Saluda, Virginia (Chesty Puller's hometown).

Our Senior School class was the first in many years to undergo language training, a choice of French or Spanish. I chose French because of an awareness of difficulties of the new South Vietnamese government following the fall of Dien Bien Phu in 1954. I had absolutely no clairvoyance that Indochina was going to erupt and that we would soon be fighting there.

Quantico armed itself with hundreds of French 101 texts, and we were immersed in daily French language classes. They quickly assigned all French-speaking Marines in the Washington, D.C., area as assistant instructors. Our instructor, Gunny Sgt. Bourbanet, helped us through the year. My brother, George, was having some difficulty with French, so we would pay a modest stipend to share our lunch with the gunny and that helped.

The wisdom of teaching the French language at the Senior School was quickly proven when less than two years later my landing force of the Sixth Fleet was assigned a French Foreign Legion parachute battalion for two months on Corsica. My French classes at the Senior School paid off.

CHAPTER 20

Battalion Commands
1965-1966

Two of us in our Senior School class were "held back" (that is, held over) to continue to serve as instructors at Senior School. Since I was late in arriving, all of the battalion commands had been assigned, so, in the interim I became the assistant G-2 intelligence officer. Col. Barney McLean, who had been my battalion commander in the Third Battalion, Fifth Marines (3/5) in Korea, was the G-2. It was a good learning experience for me, and I worked hard to do the best job possible until I was assigned command of Third Battalion, Second Marines (3/2) under Col. Charlie Brush.

Col. Brush was a great mentor and a damn fine regimental commander. He took me on a command visit to Vieques in the Caribbean where 3/2 was just finishing its Caribbean deployment. Upon return to Camp Lejeune, I took command of 3/2 and commenced training them for the next year's deployment as the Med Battalion, the landing force of the Sixth Fleet.

An Accident that Almost Led to Losing Command
of the Med Battalion

THEN FIRST LT. JOHN RIPLEY, a platoon leader in Second Force Recon, came to see me and invited me to jump with the them on my "permissive orders" that all parachute-qualified officers carry so they can occasionally jump to maintain parachute proficiency. Initially, I declined because 3/2 was scheduled to depart Moorehead City, North Carolina, for Rota, Spain, and the Sixth Fleet.

• • •

Col. John Ripley, who had invited me to jump with his platoon, later became a Navy Cross hero in Vietnam when he blew the bridge at Dong Ha. We remained close friends until his death a few years ago. I have the painting of "Ripley at the Bridge" as a treasured memory of one of the most outstanding Marine officers that I have had the pleasure to serve and jump with. The original of this five- by six-foot oil is in the Rotunda of Honor, just inside the front gate at Ripley's Naval Academy.

• • •

I finally gave in to Ripley's persistence and agreed to make one jump with his platoon. It was an unusually bitter, cold day for Camp Lejeune, and we exited the helicopter. I landed hard on the CG's frozen parade deck. I heard a pop and knew I had broken something. I limped home.

My next-door neighbor, a medical doctor, Cdr. Norm Wenger, assistant division surgeon, noted my limp. He wanted to x-ray my left leg. Doc Wenger knew that I was scheduled to deploy to the Mediterranean in ten days, and he also knew I did not want to lose command of my battalion because of a leg injury. He took me to the Naval Hospital, shooed out the corpsmen, and took his own x-rays. He advised me that I had a nondisplaced fracture of my tibial plateau and that it would heal in ten days. He told me to use a cane for that period. I did, except when I went in to meet with Maj. Gen. van Rysen for my predeployment briefings. I strode in, inwardly wincing because of the severe pain, and later went back on my cane to the Jeep. I limped for ten days, and it did heal by the time we pulled into Rota, Spain, for the assumption of command as Commander of the Landing Force Sixth Fleet. It all worked out, and I kept the battalion until we were relieved seven months later.

Our tour was supposed to be six months, but the JCS extended us one month, as they were considering sending us as a deployed landing force around east through the Suez Canal to Vietnam via the back door.

Our battalion landing team (BLT) 3/2 had an intensive and fulfilling seven months as part of the Sixth Fleet. We deployed on five ships on Amphibious Squadron 10 under Capt. Ed Miller, USN He led our naval flotilla of five ships: the USS *Monrovia* (APA 31), USS *Telfair* (APA 210), USS *Uvalde* (AKA 48), USS *Ft. Snelling* (LSD-30), and the USS *Grant* (LSD-1174).

During our seven months deployed, we reported into the Sixth Fleet at Rota Spain. Our first port of call was Marseilles, France; we later had a training landing at Aranci Bay, Sardinia; we also operated with French Commando at Santa Monza, Corsica (France). Live-firing of all weapons followed at Porto Scudo-Laspezia; later, operations with the British at Valeta, Malta, where we fired against the British International Rifle and Pistol Teams in the annual Admiral Cassady Cup. The Cassady Cup was so named for its donor, who had been a Navy admiral, commander of the Sixth Fleet. He established the Cassady Cup to "inspire and perpetuate international marksmanship by all future Med battalions." Battalion Landing team (BLT) 3/2 won the Cassady Cup and all rifle and pistol competitions. The BLT basketball team also participated in the Malta Invitational Basketball Tournament. To the surprise of the local RAF team, our BLT swept the tournament.

We conducted a port call in Naples, Italy, and then spent Christmas in Genoa. Our last stops in Italy were split with one half of us going ashore at Port Scudo-Laspezia and the other half going ashore at Livorno, both on the west coast of northern Italy. We had two days in Palma, Mallorca. Our final on-the-beach operations were two operations on Corsica with the Parachute Battalion of the French Foreign Legion on the Island of Corsica. We exchanged a parachute battalion company with India Company on Corsica. Our last port visit in Spain was to Barcelona.

In Support of Search Efforts off the Coast of Spain

DURING THE APPROACHING END to our deployment, our BLT operated in support of the search for missing atomic bombs off southern Spain. A mid-air collision over southern Spain between a loaded B-52 and its tanker caused the loss of four atomic bombs. Two landed on the beach and were quickly recovered. The JCS directed all units in the Med to assist in recovery of the missing bombs.

One of the unforeseen by-products of using our amphibious shipping to support this search of the waters of the collision site off of the Spanish coast was to use our LSD to become a "mother ship" to a deep-diving mini-submarine. Upon arrival of the minisub, I pleaded with the lieutenant commander skipper to not flood the well deck down until my unit could rebutton up their tanks while the well-deck was still dry. He refused to wait the several hours it was going to take to button up. I had to advise the Joint Chiefs of his actions. Later, I was advised that poor judgment by that skipper finished his naval career.

Damage to our tanks by premature flooding of the well deck when we were required to load the miniature submarine, *Alvin,* used in recovery of the sunken atomic bomb put us in nondeployable status until the tanks could be repaired. The flooding of our unbuttoned tanks required complete replacement of all electronic gear. This was to be done quickly at the naval base of Toulon, France. A Marine special technical team with all replacement communications gear was to be flown in from the Marine Corps repair facility at Albany, Georgia. The "missing" lost atomic bomb was then recovered by *Alvin* and all was well again with the JCS back in the United States.

When I look back on what we called our "Spanish lost-atomic-bomb operation," it evidences some of the types of problems that an officer of Marines encounters, thousands of miles away from his parent Marine division encounters. Those actions might involve, as in this situation, the governments of two nations, foreign services, and the full spectrum of U.S. Armed Forces.

We returned to the States at Moorhead City, North Carolina, tired, but now far more experienced, satisfied with a "Well Done" from our Sixth Fleet commanding general and admiral.

CHAPTER 21

The Naval War College
1966-1967

Returning from the Med quickly finished my three years at Camp Lejeune and sent us on orders to Newport, Rhode Island, to the senior course at the Naval War College. The course was great, and we had good classmates. As a family, we spent a lot of time swimming, diving for lobster in the fall, and sailing out from Narragansett Bay into the Atlantic toward Brenton Reef Light. With regret, we sold our sailboat to get ready for Vietnam. There was great emphasis, at the time, on advanced degrees and all of our classmates that did not have them were urged to earn them.

The president of the Navy War College, Vice Adm. Tom "Chick" Hayward, called three of us into his office for a short conference. He told us: "I see you three officers all had the foresight to obtain your advanced degrees, I am not going to let you sit around with your feet up on your desks while your classmates are busting their tails to get what you already have. I had dinner with the president of Brown University (an Ivy League university twenty-five miles up the road from Newport). I have arranged for the three of you to join a masters/doctoral program at Brown for Chinese international relations." Since each of us had been to China, he felt that it was appropriate for all of us to enlighten some of the more liberal Brown students. We made the best of it, and my paper, "Chinese Hegemony," was published by the *Navy War College Review*. The three of us—Army Lt. Col. Dick Stauffer;

Navy Cmdr. Dick Patton; and me, a Marine lieutenant colonel—all ended up as distinguished graduates of the senior officers' course at the Naval War College. All of us were off to Vietnam. Shortly after our graduation, both lieutenant colonels made 0-6 and Cmdr. Patton made captain, quickly followed by promotion to rear admiral.

Our class was exposed to returning military commanders and other government leaders who were surprisingly candid in sharing their views on current events. I was not surprised to be asked to join the luncheon table with Admiral Hayward and our speaker of the day, the then-Secretary of State.

Our class in the senior course at the Navy War College was a mix of men from all of the services (no women at that point in time). We had about eight Marines, all lieutenant colonels or colonels, about forty senior Navy officers, about fifteen senior Army officers, about ten senior air force officers, and one coast guard officer. Virtually every member of our class was on orders to Vietnam in June 1967. All of us were given thirty days leave.

OUR THREE BOYS had enjoyed Newport. The schools were good. None of our boys had any school problems later when they adjusted into our Seattle school system.

I got to know my neighbor in student housing, who was assigned to be a torpedo recovery officer for all naval facilities in the Narragansett Bay/Newport Harbor area. He invited my boys and me to go diving on weekends for lobster. We frequently had fresh lobster and wine on Sunday afternoons with some of our classmates. What a life. Because of the fun that we were having diving for lobster, I was able to keep my qualifications as a Marine Corps diver current. The academic year went quickly, and then I was off to march to the sound of guns in Vietnam.

CHAPTER 22

To Vietnam
1967-1968

Upon reporting to the Ninth MEB (Marine Expeditionary Brigade) located on Okinawa, I became the G-3, operations officer of the brigade, to now-Brig. Gen. Bill Chipp. We had served together on Okinawa, when, as a lieutenant colonel, he commanded 1/9 on Okinawa. Our major infantry unit, the Twenty-Sixth Marine Regiment, was deployed in-country in Vietnam.

Previously selected for colonel after graduating from the Navy War College, I relieved Dave Lownds as G-3, and he left to assume command of the Twenty-sixth Marine Regiment in-country. I commuted to our Vietnam units by C-130 Marine transport for about five months until I took command of Special Landing Force Alpha, landing force of the Seventh Fleet, after I put my "eagles" on in January 1968. My new command, the SLF, was making landings on the Vietnam coast from the demilitarized zone (DMZ) at the Cua Viet River, south to the Chu Lai area near Da Nang, both locations were generally along the middle of the Vietnam coast.

My landing force was headquartered on the LPH *Iwo Jima*. A number of infantry battalions from in-country and a number of different helicopter squadrons rotated through my landing force for the next four months, one BLT and one H34 squadron per month. In early April, I received a scrambled message, coded to prevent listening by our North Vietnamese enemy, for me to take command of the Twenty-Sixth

Marines at Khe Sanh. I remember that it was 0300 hours when I received the call. I woke my staff and the BLT and squadron commanders, thanked them for their service, and said goodbye. I was piped with sideboys boarding one of our SLF choppers, a Sikorsky H-34, with a brief stop at Dong Ha to get any final orders.

Gen. Rathvon McClure Tompkins, CG Third Marine Division, and I were in Khe Sanh by 1100 hours that day.

CHAPTER 23

Khe Sanh
1968

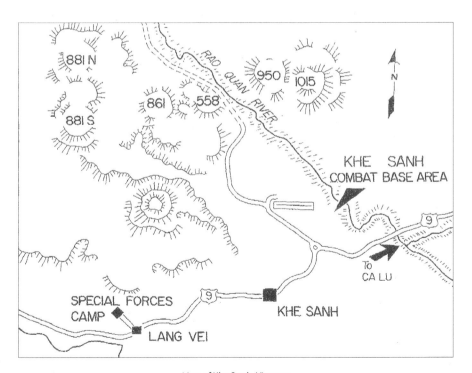

Map of Khe Sanh, Vietnam.

Col. Bruce Meyers.
At the time that the author assumed command at Khe Shan,
he was the youngest full colonel (O-6) in the Marine Corps.

On April 12, 1968 I took command of the regiment. I had been at Khe Sanh many times before and during the eighty-plus-day siege as the G-3/operations officer of the Ninth Marine Brigade.

The defense of Khe Sanh was now my responsibility and, as the new commander, I wanted to walk the lines. The change of command ceremony was very abbreviated. Basically, they took a picture of Col. Dave Lownds handing me the flag, symbolic of the actual change of command. We saluted, and I spoke the traditional words, "I relieve you, sir," and then we all ran to get under cover for the incoming that our brief gathering had generated.

Khe Sanh change of command, April 12, 1968.

Walking the Lines

BEFORE RECOUNTING MY WALKING THE LINES, it is appropriate for me to briefly describe the makeup of my new regiment. I had a total of 6,300 troops, mostly Marines, two Navy elements (a detachment from a USN construction battalion, CBs, and a well-manned Navy surgical element), a small USAF control element, and other assorted odds and bods. My command of the regiment now included having five Marine Corps Infantry Battalions, 1/26, 2/26, 3/26, and 1/9 as my four infantry battalions; 1/13 was my artillery battalion; and Third ARVN Ranger Battalion. It also included our small but well equipped mini-emergency hospital called Charlie Med. This facility was manned by ten to twelve Navy surgeons of every possible discipline: thoracic surgeons, cardiologists, dentists, orthopedists, ophthalmologists, neurologists, a psychiatrist, including a number of corpsmen as my primary medical element to handle immediate medical emergencies. Emergency medical evacuations (medevacs) were constantly sending our wounded south to Da Nang and to our hospital there.

With this information as background, I took my regimental Sgt. Maj. Agrippa Smith, an impressive six-foot-four sergeant, on this walk of the lines. One of my chaplains, Lt. Father Bernard Filmyer, who had served with me a year before in the

Mediterranean when I commanded the landing force of the Sixth Fleet, asked to come along. I was delighted to have Father Filmyer serving with me again. We were going west down the airstrip, walking on the pierced aluminum matting. First, I was going to visit the troops from 1/26, under the command of Lt. Col. Fred McEwan, who were manning our perimeter on the extreme eastern edge of Khe Sanh Combat Base. In crossing the airstrip and moving east toward the lines of 1/26, one did not tarry. You moved quickly and purposefully since the North Vietnamese were constantly observing the Marine activity within our lines. Not only did they have well-trained snipers, but their artillery and rocket elements had observers who would call in fire on anyone that they observed above ground as potential targets.

We were not running, but we were moving pretty quickly to keep from being live targets for their snipers, rockets, and artillery. We were about seventy-five yards from 1/26's easternmost defensive lines when the North Vietnamese near to Long Vei (just across the Laotian border) began to walk rocket fire down the airstrip trying to catch us in the open. We all sprinted to the lines and dove down into the defensive trench, ending up on top of two Marines who, at that moment, were heating their evening C-ration cup of joe. The two frontline 1/26 Marines were naturally startled and did not expect to be landed on by three running intruders in their domain.

We had on our helmets and flak jackets. When in combat, officers and enlisted seldom wear rank insignia, in order to not set us apart as special target. I don't remember discussing whether we would wear some form of insignia since we were going to be walking the lines. In any event, Father Filmyer was wearing a small gold cross in the middle of his flak jacket. I was wearing a small silver colonel's insignia covered with duct tape and, as I remember, Sgt. Maj. Smith was wearing a small regimental sergeant major's insignia.

Having just had their carefully heated evening coffee dumped, both Marines were ticked and turned to vent their anger on the intruders. The first Marine had just started to curse Father Filmyer when he stopped midsentence after he finally noticed the chaplain's cross. Next, he fiercely turned to me but quickly spotted my colonel's insignia, with its duct tape now removed. In desperation, he turned to the third coffee dumper, Sgt. Maj. Smith, to vent his anger. At that point, he gave up his intended rant and said something like, "Jesus Christ, first it's the chaplain, then the old man, our new regimental commander (me), and then it's our regimental sergeant major. How can we win?"

In combat, when you are receiving incoming fire, you will frequently turn to talking about totally unrelated things, I suppose to keep your mind off the realities of the incoming fire. I remember that moment after the coffee incident when Father

Filmyer and I started talking about innocuous memories of our times in the Med together. We briefly spoke of visiting the Pope's palace at Avignon, north of Marseilles. The Marines both spoke up in awe, commenting on how their new regimental commander and their chaplain had obviously served together over a year before, a half world away. Somehow the incongruity of that moment broke the tension and all five of us had a good laugh about it.

The Day-to-Day of Commanding a Regiment Under Siege

MY STYLE OF LEADERSHIP may or may not have been the same as some of my peers. While commanding my battalion, I tried to get out with my four rifle companies on a daily basis, if possible. Generally, I would take my operations officer (S-3) and sometimes my battalion intelligence officer (S-2) with me on my rounds of the battalion. I quickly found that in Khe Sanh, with five Marine Corps battalions and one Vietnamese battalion under my direct command, my time with my subordinate units became an instant problem. I should explain that my approach as a commander to my subordinate units was to express confidence in the leadership of their units. I was aware from other regiments I had served in that there was a fine line of trust and an awareness and that a tiny step over the lines during my almost daily visits could possibly be viewed as a lack of trust in their leadership. I backed off and decided to never cross that line. As regimental commander, I kept asking myself and my staff what could be done to make us more successful in our jobs. I wanted to help but not come across as trying to unduly influence the subordinate's command of his unit.

Communication becomes the key to success. Each of the twenty or more officers who made up my regimental staff was communicating with their counterparts. As the regimental commander, I was in contact with our Third Marine Division staff, twenty to twenty-five miles west, at the coastal town of Dong Ha, located on the demilitarized zone (DMZ). Our radios had scramblers so that the enemy could not listen in on our conversation. Transmissions would be scrambled by technology and unscrambled at the division headquarters, because both sides, the United States and the North Vietnamese, had intelligence personnel who were listening twenty-four hours a day. This required a fairly sophisticated staff, highly qualified communicators and interpreters who could make sense of traffic from our enemy, the North Vietnamese.

Our S-1 handled all administrative matters such as names of all replacements or lists of the wounded or casualties from each of the five Marine battalions in my command. My intelligence officer was in daily contact with his counterpart in the G-2, the intelligence officer for the Third Marine Division; Lt. Col. Roger Hagerty, my S-3, gathered orders and all kinds of information on operations underway or planned for the future. My logistics officer, Maj. Buck Lumpkin, was ensuring that we had enough "beans and bullets" left to stay operational and keep our weapons with adequate artillery shells and other ammunition. Suffice it to say, important communication was going on at all times that literally involved our entire regimental staff.

Our air officer and his staff were constantly evaluating our complex aerial supply traffic. Air controllers were constantly coordinating the arrival and departure of all resupply aircraft, the C-130s and C-123s filled with cargo and replacements. They were also arranging for various types of helicopters and attack aircraft to support our forces.

Aerial Delivery of Supplies Using LAPES Extraction

KHE SANH AIRSTRIP made substantial usage of an Army/air force developed delivery method called LAPES (Low Altitude Parachute Proximity Extraction System). Wooden pallets were loaded with all manner of gear: rations, artillery and weapon ammunition, as well as medical and blood supplies—virtually anything that we could lash securely to the pallet came in on our LAPES extraction system. The crew chief or loadmaster of the usual transport-type aircraft Lockheed C-130E Hercules would, on order from the aircraft commander, release the pallets, while simultaneously pulling the ripcord on a moderate-sized parachute. The moment that this parachute filled with air from our aircraft's speed and the slipstream, it would literally pull the pallets secured together and they would "clean out the cargo area of the aircraft" within seconds of releasing the pallets and parachute. During the winter and spring, Khe Sanh was in the clouds a lot of the time. It was a very moist atmosphere and we had our share of rain and muggy monsoon weather. This made the pierced aluminum runway very slick and slippery. In most cases, the loaded pallets would drop the short distance (two to three feet) and thunder down the runway, slowing down as they came. The majority of time, these fast-moving wooden pallets, heavily loaded, would continue going in the same direction as the aircraft. Occasionally, one or more of the pallets would skew to one side of the runway and damage anything they hit. If there was any delay in pulling the parachute or releasing the pallets, the point where they hit the runway surface late was close to the eastern end of the runway edge.

This had a tragic consequence shortly before I arrived. Several pallets of heavy artillery shells landed late trying to slow down from the speed of almost a hundred miles per hour at time of drop. They thundered down the monsoon rain-slicked runway into a small, stand-up mess hall, killing two Marines. The speeding late-drop pallets had gone into the area at the end of the paved area of the airstrip that aviators called the overrun area. Having been an FAA-licensed and active general-aviation pilot for twenty-four years, I was very familiar with overrun areas that are at either end of an active runway. As soon as I heard about this accident at Khe Sanh, I ordered an immediate closing and moving of that mess hall. I spoke to my regimental air officer and directed him to review the overrun area for anything that could be damaged by the pallets and move them to safer locations. This is a brief overview of the intensity of our day-to-day activities during the siege.

Gaggles and Super Gaggles

ONE LESSON LEARNED about maintaining the high ground in the surrounding hills was the absolute necessity of getting helicopters in and out every day, sometimes several times a day. The number of helicopters shot down rose in January 1968. This led to the development of a "Gaggle" and later a "Super Gaggle." The Gaggle grew out of use of the A-4 Skyhawks and pretty typical coordination and cooperation between infantry officers and aviators working together to solve a problem. Marines in Vietnam worked together to solve the heavy losses of helicopters arriving and departing from units maintaining a combat patrol/fire base at locations that were virtually surrounded by North Vietnamese forces. This was pretty typical in our units in the hills occupied around Khe Sanh Combat Base.

The A-4 Skyhawk fighter/bombers were the aircraft initially chosen to provide continuing support to the resupply of isolated hill outposts. The A-4s would make a series of runs firing suppressing fire and dropping some bombs. After the suppression fires, the A-4 would smoke a corridor with the fire base in the center. We knew that they had our usual LZs pretty well pre-sited. The smoke sprayed from these small A-4 aircraft kept them from having sufficient visibility to adjust these preplanned enemy fires.

The Vietnamese were using 12.5mm (50 caliber) antiaircraft machine guns supplemented by their normal infantry weapon fire. This combined fire of Vietnamese antiaircraft fire added to by emplaced infantry units initially proved quite effective for the Vietnamese. The helos would fly down the corridor with the A-4s suppressing to the sides. The helicopters would touch down for as short a period as possible, drop their load, and instantly load and take off. Some pilots and crews kept their on-the-ground time to about thirty to forty-five seconds. Our helicopter pilots reported that they received about the same amount of fire once they off-loaded and departed, flying out the corridor, as they had on the inbound run.

The Super Gaggle grew out from the original Gaggle. Our aviators began to increase the number of A-4s from four to twelve and concentrated the A-4s on flak suppression. The number of helicopters went up in a like matter to massed flights of twelve to sixteen helicopters, but the basic flight patterns and corridor remained essentially the same. Casualties of our supply helicopters began to drop whenever the resupply could be done simultaneously at two or three such locations.

With twenty-four or more different aircraft flying around the same airspace, it took a great deal of very careful coordination to avoid midair collisions. We grunts thanked God and the Marine Corps for having such skilled pilots who rose to the occasion. Monsoon weather and low ceilings made all flying exceedingly demanding to say the least.

By the end of February 1968, the Super Gaggle proved to be the turning point and as the weather began clearing in March, the daily delivery to these hill stations rose to over forty tons per day. The source describing the Super Gaggle tactic was the Marine Corps monograph, *The Battle of Khe Sanh*. In addition to my own observations, more of the data on LAPES came from C-123 pilot and Medal of Honor recipient Col. Joe Jackson, my friend and a fellow member of the Seattle Hanger of Quiet Birdmen.[1]

• • •

When one writes books and articles, there is a tendency to focus somewhat on our most recent experiences. In looking back on my first two books, Fortune Favors the Brave *and* Swift, Silent, and Deadly, *I sense that my focus was on the historical, equipment, and problem solving with relation to parachutes and submarine operations. My later writings reflect several significant differences. First, at the time I was two ranks more senior (colonel vs. major); second, by then I had been a brigade G-2 intelligence officer (Second MarDiv), later a brigade G-3 operations officer (Ninth MAB in Vietnam) and finally, commander of two landing forces (Sixth Fleet and Seventh Fleet), as well as a regimental commander in combat for five months. Each of these interim assignments, I am sure, impacted my approach and my writing.*

• • •

---

1 Quiet Birdmen is a social group of pilots who meet monthly in all major cities to talk about airplanes.

BACK TO KHE SANH: We were being hit by rocket and artillery fire on our airstrip. Each hit generally blew a hole in the pierced aluminum matting that made up our runway. We had small teams of Navy construction battalions on both sides and along our runway. They had small cutting torches and mallets and would quickly cut out the damaged matting and replace it as soon as it was damaged. They were incredibly brave and were frequently being rocketed and mortared upon while they worked. A count was made of each rocket and mortar round as it landed. Our artillery units calculated the direction of fire and tried to locate the enemy's firing positions for counterbattery fire. On many days, our combat base would receive over one thousand enemy rounds during the day. Clearly, my North Vietnamese opponent, Gen. Vo Nguyen Giap, was trying to replicate his defeat of the French forces at Dien Bien Phu in 1954.[2] Gen. Giap passed away in late 2013.

I benefited from having the experience that I gained from other field operations, including my thirteen months of combat in 1950 and 1951 in Korea, a good part of which was as a rifle company commander. The intensity of activity at Khe Sanh dictated that I plan my day to either communicate with each battalion commander, make a command visit by helicopter, or use "shanks mare" (on foot).

Looking back, some of these command visits were pretty hairy. They required good timing and quick exit by chopper. Every battle site with one of my unit's locations was constantly being observed by our enemy. Frequently, our choppers would land, take some wounded aboard, and be off the ground again in under thirty seconds. Neither our brave pilots nor I and my staff wanted to tarry on our LZ or we would become an instant target. In and out quickly was the watchword.

---

2   (See Peter McDonald's *The Victor in Vietnam: Giap* (Norton Press, NY, 1993).

CHAPTER 24

Operations Outside of the Wire
1968

Col. Lownds and I, as then current commander of Khe Sanh, had been operating under a constraint from the Joint Chiefs of Staff, as well as CG III MAF and Maj. Gen. Tompkins, that kept us from using our defensive posture in any manner to start offensive action outside of our defensive lines. This restriction was lifted, and Gen. Tompkins advised it would be appropriate to conduct offensive operations outside our lines now.

Following the Air Cav's aggressive move up Route 9 from the coast and the Da Nang areas, many war correspondents and Army historians were expecting some sort of official recognition that "the siege had been broken" by the actions of the First Cav. Let me quickly add that none of our Marines or corpsmen felt that the Air Cav's coming up Route 9 was any major thing. This does not mean that our Marines were not appreciative of the Air Cav's assault. We welcomed them, but each of us Marines felt that our defense of Khe Sanh had been done in a professional manner. More probably than not, we could not have done it without the tremendous exterior support in air strikes that we got from the air force's forty-five specialized ARC Light B-52 bombers, which decimated Gen. Giap's Vietnamese forces. Again, we probably could not have held Khe Sanh without the other terrific air support provided by the 1,625 tactical sorties by the other services: U.S. Air Force from in-country and

The author at Khe Sanh.

U.S. Navy aircraft from carriers six hundred fifty sorties by Marine aviation, the four hundred thirty-six sorties flown by carrier aircraft from Task Force 77, and the seventy-seven other sorties by ARVN[1] and U.S. Army aircraft. Before writing this, I checked on enemy casualties. It was estimated that with our ARC Light (specialized aerial bombing) B-52 raids and all other air strikes, we killed an estimated eleven thousand five hundred enemy troops during this two-month period of "the siege." I personally would have to conclude that it was the combination of a determined six battalions and our great air power assets that kept Khe Sanh from falling. I feel that I now have a better understanding why these casualties suffered by Giap's forces were very severe to the North Vietnamese ability to carry on the fight in South Vietnam near and around Khe Sanh. I feel that for these reasons, our POWs in the Hanoi Hilton were buoyed by the outcome.

THE LACK OF ANY CELEBRATING of an end of the siege was clearly acknowledged in the official document describing the relief up Route 9 by the Air Cav under Gen. Tolson. Traditionally, the lifting of a siege has been the occasion for great emotional outbursts, bands, and stirring oration. In this regard, Khe Sanh was somewhat of a disappointment. Gen. Tolson, CG of First Air Cav, wanted the

1   ARVN: Army of the Republic of Vietnam.

linkup to be with a minimum of fanfare so that he could get the Marines on the offensive again.[2]

Gen. Tompkins flew up to Khe Sanh on an official command visit and asked my opinion on what actions we could take outside the wire. I immediately recommended a limited battalion-sized attack by my Third Battalion, Twenty-Sixth Marines. Lt. Col. John Studt's 3/26 held the southern of two twin terrain massifs (881 South and 881 North) facing toward the north-northwest from Khe Sanh Combat Base. I recommended adoption of Col. Studt's plan to Gen. Tompkins that the 3/26 be tasked with the retaking of Hill 881 North. Tompkins agreed that was the logical next move for us to take. Hill 881 North was currently occupied by a North Vietnamese battalion with the strength of about 350 North Vietnamese.

Col. Studt and I had known each other for years; the history of our former contacts was stunning on reflection. Studt had been a PFC (private first class) in my rifle company in the Korean War serving in H/3/5 in 1951 in the mountainous terrain above the Thirty-Eighth parallel north of Yangu and Inje. We were both wounded about the same time. He was medevaced and went back to the United States, where he was discharged and returned to college. Upon graduation, he immediately took a commission in the Marine Corps and was promoted through the years until he ended up as one of my battalion commanders in the 3/26 at Khe Sanh. Hollywood's central casting could not have come up with a more improbable circumstance than what true history had given us. Col. Studt and I discussed a basic plan and agreed to our planned direct attack up Hill 881 North. I directed my air officer, a major, to lay on every available bit of air support that they could: Marine Corps, U.S. Navy Task Force 77, and U.S. Air Force. He did, and, at dawn, they were stacked overhead. Studt decided to leave elements of one of his rifle companies to hold 881 South under Capt. Bill Dabney, who had just been selected for promotion to major. I flew up to be on 881 South with Dabney to provide close regimental support to his attack. I frequently did this in order to give immediate assistance, not to look over his shoulder. Sometimes in combat it is meaningful to get as close as you can without interfering unnecessarily.

Col. Studt quietly led two of his remaining rifle companies out of the wire at midnight. They made their way north down to a small river that ran east-west between hills 881 South and 88 North. He chose this river, easily recognized in the dark, to be his line of departure. They started up the southern slopes of Hill 881 North at about 0530; the sun was just coming up. Air strikes simultaneously began to hit the

---

2 Gen. Tolson had previously been given operational control of the three brigades of the Air Cavalry Division (ACD)—the Twenty-Sixth Marines, the First Marines, and the Third ARVN Airborne Task Force—in early April 1968. Thus, the description of how the aircraft's actions were to be handled.

northern side of 881 North. During the prior eighty-plus days of the siege, 3/26 had assembled about eight 106 recoilless rifles gathered from other locations around its perimeter. They were hub-to-hub and a seasoned "gunny" was firing them under Capt. Dabney's orders. It became a killing barrage that was impacting just forward of the advancing Col. Studt and the remainder of the battalion. This "overhead close" barrage was walking up Hill 881 North, just ahead of the advancing troops. It was beautifully coordinated. If anyone came into view ahead of the advancing 3/26, the Vietnamese or scrub trees were just being blown away. The troops were using this advance as payback time. Maj. Matt Caulfield (he would later be promoted to major general), the S-3, radioed me and advised that "they were fixing bayonets and overrunning the crest of Hill 881 North." He advised me that "the lead attacking troops had just taken off on their own and were overrunning the hill. I could not stop them." (These are actual quotes from Caulfeld to me via his field radio.)

Remnants of the previously occupying North Vietnamese battalion were pouring out of the back of the crest of Hill 881 North, trying to escape. The forward air controllers with Studt's battalion continued to call "danger close air strikes"[3] on these Vietnamese troops, making a last-ditch effort to get away from the seemingly unstoppable overrunning by lead elements of 3/26. They were all killed. In my postaction report, I described this assault as I have just written it. In the official monograph, pg.143, I described observing one of the attacking Marines scramble up one of the scrub trees still standing at the top of Hill 881 North, pause, and pull a small American Stars and Stripes out of his pack and attach it to the scrub remnant tree. Sgt. Stryker of the movie *Sands of Iwo Jima* could not have had a more dramatic end to this superb limited assault. This successful limited assault was followed by the planned withdrawal of all our forces on Hill 881 North back to Hill 881 South to await our orders to evacuate Khe Sanh Combat Base, with temporary responsibility assumed by the First Marine regiment which had just begun to arrive at Khe Sanh for the relief of my regiment.

Lt. Col. John "Blacky" Cahill, CO of the First Battalion, and the Ninth Marines Company wanted their chance at payback. He told me his plans to take Hill 689, to the west of 1/9's current positions. I asked if he needed any help on any phase of his attack. He declined because he felt comfortable with his own plans and their intent to use his artillery in support. Blacky used two of his companies in trail, with A Company in the lead followed by C Company, and D Company bringing up the rear.

A Company 1/9 under Capt. Henry Banks began to receive what was perceived as sniper fire. He set up a base of fire and continued up the hill. The time was about

---

3   The term "danger close" is the term Marines use for air or artillery that is being fired extremely close to friendly troops.

1000 hours. Banks deployed his Second Platoon to suppress the sniper fire that was thought to be holding up the first platoon. Unfortunately, A Company had run into a heavily fortified and well-camouflaged U-shaped reverse slope ambush and took immediate heavy casualties. Lt. Michael Hayden, commanding the Second platoon was killed in action (KIA) immediately. Two other team members were wounded, and the platoon sergeant, Sgt. Rice, was killed. Clearly, the Vietnamese had carefully withheld major return fire until the attempted envelopment of the right side of the U-shaped defense. They opened fire with vengeance and, in short order, A Company was fully engaged and suffered ten KIA and many more wounded in their blooding[4]. Cahill moved C Company on the right where A Company had hit the right side. He then tried to shift the attack to the left side of the U-shaped ambush. Capt. Hummer was badly wounded, as were two of his remaining platoon leaders. Several squad leaders were wounded about this same time, further reducing the effectiveness of C Company. Artillery counterbattery fire was called in as well as air strikes. The AO-directed air strikes failed to diminish the ambush. At this point, Cahill committed his reserve D Company in trace behind both C and A. Cahill sent D Company to again attack the right north side of the ambush. He failed to notify regiment at the Twenty-Sixth Marines of the deployment of his reserve. This was about midday, at 1200 hours. Unfortunately, there was a failure to recognize the reverse-slope U-shaped ambush for what it was. His deployments to either side of what we knew to be a well-constructed and camouflaged ambush, although aggressive, and his continuing attacks against an obvious superior force were absolutely wrong. Each of his deployments sustained very heavy casualties, and Cahill himself was wounded. He displayed incredible bravery, placing himself in harm's way. His battalion appeared unable to continue any attack. The battalion exec took over, and, for the first time at about 1500 hours, gave notice to me, the regimental commander, of the disastrous midmorning encounter with the U-shaped defense.

I choppered in, quickly assessed the situation, and brought the wounded Cahill back to be cared for. I had the rest of 1/9 withdraw, bringing in their dead and wounded as best they could, casualties sustained despite Cahill's best efforts. I briefed Gen. Tompkins on Cahill's situation. He sent Col. Wally Cuenin, who was on Tompkins' staff, to investigate what happened.

It is always difficult to look back when evaluating combat to determine what happened. I felt badly about the outcome, particularly since the 3/26 attack had been so successful the day before. Gen. Tompkins immediately relieved Col. Cahill of command of his 1/9 battalion. I had been regimental commander for just three

---

4   A self-describing term indicating severe casualties from an aggressive attack.

days with Cahill's 1/9 as part of my regiment, so this was not a case of the regimental commander's failure to properly monitor his subordinates. I was aware that Cahill had been commissioned following a strong career as a gunnery sergeant. Marine Corps schools drill it into the head of all of its students—whether they are lieutenants, captains, colonels, or even former gunnery sergeants—never to commit your reserve without advising the next commander up the chain of command. In the many times I have looked back at 1/9's performance on Hill 689, I finally have concluded that despite Col. Cahill's schooling in tactics at Quantico, he failed to recognize in a timely manner the reverse-slope horseshoe ambush for what it was. With the severe intensity of fire at the outset and the obvious sniper fire on all visible leaders, he should not have committed the remainder of his battalion in the piecemeal commitments that decimated his battalion. The Marine Corps University and I, as a former instructor at Senior School, would first ask him to withdraw, regroup, get additional firepower and air strikes on the enemy, and, only then, continue the attack. Cahill failed to keep me, his regimental commander, fully informed and, I being unaware that he had committed all of his reserves until 1500 hours during an attack that started at 1000 hours, he exhibited poor judgment. I learned much from these first two battalion attacks outside the wire. I continued command of the Twenty-Sixth Marines for the remaining five months of my deployment. We had a number of engagements that all proved very successful. I never had an incident of this nature happen again, but I surely learned from it. I felt blessed six months later because, when I returned for duty at Marine Corps schools, I became exec and later commanding officer of the Basic School. I could assure myself that, as long as I was at the Marine Corps Schools, every student officer would know to keep the next senior in command aware of the status of their unit and the sanctity of not committing the reserves piecemeal.

Withdrawal of the Twenty-Sixth Marines from Khe Sanh

FOLLOWING ORDERS TO WITHDRAW FROM KHE SANH, I initially took the Twenty-Sixth Marines by helicopter down to the coast on the Tonkin Gulf near Quang Tri. At that moment, we were a regiment without much in the way of equipment. We had lost equipment and left damaged equipment in the rubble at Khe Sanh for destruction with the rest of the base. Much of our weaponry had to be replaced, and new weapons and equipment had to be reissued so that we could operate. Virtually all the pieces in our First Battalion Thirteenth Marines Division was shot out during the siege. There were no replacements for any of our guns. They had been fired so much that their tubes were worn out and they were no longer safe to fire. The generators, trucks, and other items that make up the equipment of a Marine infantry regiment had to be replaced. Our regiment took the brunt of anger and frustration from most of the other battalion and regimental commanders in both the Third and First Marine Divisions. They were fueled by their ire at losing their spare artillery pieces, mortars, trucks, generators, and other equipment, virtually every one of the artillery pieces in our First Battalion Thirteenth Marines Division was shot out during the siege. It took about three weeks to get back to full armament, but both our generals were experienced and knew what we needed to fight. We received trucks from both First and Third Motor Transport, tanks from both tank battalions. Literally all of our replacement gear came from fellow Marines in other units deployed within Vietnam.

About this time, Gen. Tompkins was relieved at the end of his tour and returned to the States for a well-deserved rest. The stress of the last six months in-country had impacted him physically. Maj. Gen. Ray "Razor" Davis came in as his relief as the new commander of the Third Marine Division. I found him to be very supportive during the few operations that we worked for him. As the new commanding general Third Marine Division, he was terrific. He was always ready to listen, and each regimental commander looked to him for the leadership that he always displayed. Upon completion of his tour in-country, Gen. Davis returned to Quantico as a three-star. He was a mentor to me, yet he never gave any favors. My wife and I considered Razor and his wife our friends.

CHAPTER 25

Lessons Learned
1968

Somehow, I was able to get through most of my list of things that influenced me, but I passed right by three items that I wish to share. My feelings of imparting certain lessons learned would not be complete without them. They relate to my being asked to take my regiment under triple canopy and operate where few Marines had recently operated. None of these incidents are that important by themselves, but let me tell you about them. We were using CH-46 Sea Knight helicopters to carry in our troops and supplies into the triple canopy. The CH-46 needs a landing zone (LZ) of two-hundred-foot cleared diameter from the jungle top to the jungle floor to land.

Peaveys Used to Help Clear Landing Zones (LZs)

IT BECAME TOO DIFFICULT to try to find landing zones near where we were to operate on Charlie Ridge, southwest of Da Nang. It quickly became apparent that we would have to perfect our ability to make our own LZs where we needed them, rather than to search for one that might do. Initially, our engineers used standard chain saws and cut the two-hundred-foot space needed to land the CH-46. Jungle trees can be difficult to make fall in the right direction. We found that we could clear a circle that was two-hundred feet in diameter, but the trees were clustered together, making it difficult to clear the jungle floor into a neat, round LZ of the appropriate space and size. Having spent a bit of time in the woods in the Northwest, first as a fire lookout in 1942, and later as a national park ranger, I knew how to use a logger's tool called a peavey. Peaveys made the job of clearing LZs much more manageable and efficient. Previously, it took us half a day to a day to cut the diameter of the LZ. It then took more than two days to clear the LZ of the mish-mash of fallen trees. Peaveys have an oak handle that is about four inches thick and five feet long. There is a steel metal spike at one end, and about eight to ten inches up from the spike is a metal hook at the end of an arm. The spike at the lower end of the handle is jammed into the log; then the hook, which is movable, is jammed into the log some distance from the spike. This gives the logger the leverage necessary to roll the log. Two loggers roll the log together, a logger at each end of maybe a ten-foot log, so they can roll the log easily in any direction. With practice, all of our LZ clearing crews quickly learned how to clear the spaces and move the logs into piles. We got a whole host of peaveys, ten as I remember.

My Second Lesson Learned Was Use of Patrol Dogs

I FIRST LEARNED TO WORK with patrol dogs in British North Borneo. We were on a Southeast Asia Treaty Organization (SEATO) landing operation north of the town of Jesselton in heavy triple canopy jungle. The unit operating with us was from New Zealand. Many of the dog handlers were Maori natives. They like working with dogs, and they do a great job. Most of the dogs I have used in combat were German shepherds. They are big, intelligent, and turned their patrol duties into a game. As we made our way through the jungle, most unit leaders placed the dog and handler up near the point. The dogs get to know who our friendlies are by their smell. The enemy has a different smell, and finding the enemy is the primary mission. When patrol dogs smell the enemy, they are trained to make a silent alert. The handler is skilled at reading his dog, and he quietly alerts his patrol leader of the approach of enemy based upon the dog's sense of smell and training. The last thing you want is a patrol dog that barks when he/she picks up the scent of the enemy. They are trained to be quiet and discreet in their work.

As a regimental commander, I asked Gen. Robertson to get some U.S. Army-trained patrol dogs for our unit. There are other types of trained dogs, such as narcotics- or explosive-smelling dogs, but for triple canopy use, the patrol dog was the best choice. At the end of two months in nothing but triple canopy by infantry patrols on foot, I ended up having sixteen patrol dogs working with my two leading canopy battalions from my Twenty-Sixth Marine regiment. It takes a while to get used to having patrol dogs in the unit, but once everyone is acclimated, they do not want to patrol without their dogs in their lead rifle companies. The dogs must be kept well-watered and fed. The handlers know that their lives depend on the dogs, so they give them the best of care. Gen. Robertson called me and asked if I knew that I had sixteen patrol dogs. I acknowledged that I did know that. He said, "Those are more patrol dogs than in the entire rest of my Marine division." I politely but quickly responded, "Gen., as long as I have had those dogs, I have not lost a Marine under triple canopy to ambush." He quickly added, "I know what you are doing and if you need more, I will get them." In re-reading this it sounds as if I was a bit impertinent. I was not. He had worked with me before in the Second MarDiv when he was a brigadier; we got along well, and we trusted each other. He was just sharing with me that we had been pretty successful using those dogs.

My use of our dogs changed our tactics a bit when we were moving west toward the Laotian border. Every article that I have read on triple canopy operations in high jungle, particularly when operating in the mountains, said to never use the game trails that run up the center of each ridgeline along the top of the ridge. Most American units operating in Vietnam ran the ridges or used the game trails that always topped most ridges. Animals always take the easy way in traversing jungle. It is easier for animals to go in a straight line to get from point A to point B. Americans in Vietnam, other than Marines who had been trained in jungle ops, will frequently follow the animals' method and run the ridges. Both the VC and NVA units were fully aware of the propensity of Americans to run the ridges. They became most adept at setting up what many tacticians called a reverse slope horseshoe defense. This is a U-shaped formation with the closed end of the U facing downhill, the open end uphill, for escape by the ambush force, once the ambush is sprung. My tactics in taking Charlie Ridge were never to use the ridgeline, when possible. Always go up a ridge hugging the side of the ridge, usually about halfway down. Usually there were creeks or small jungle rivers occupying the low ground at the bottom edge of the ridge line moving inland. It was more difficult travel for the troops to move inland on the flanks of the ridge line, but we took our time and used the dogs to keep from being ambushed, using the sides of ridges. I remember that it took us about two days of traveling inland on the midside of the ridges, staying always off the ridge crest with its typical game trail. Then, we would ascend the ridge line to the crest, turn back in the opposite direction, and literally run down the game trail using a dog and handler with our lead runners keenly looking forward and down the hill for signs of the Vietnamese ambush site. We would come in on the back of their U-shaped proposed ambush site where they were waiting for us to ascend the ridge line. The patrol dogs always alerted us as we came downhill to roll up the rear of their ambush site. We ended up counterambushing three or four such potential North Vietnamese ambushes by using what my S-3 began to call "our buttonhook" assaults. Every time we buttonhooked, we got good kills and captured virtually all weapons.

Sophisticated Helicopter Forced Down by Ancient French Hunting Rifle

SOME READING THIS will accuse me of merely writing a sea story. This occurred when I was operating with my Twenty-Sixth Marine Regiment around May or June of 1968. The regiment was sharing Hill 55 SW to the east of Da Nang with the First Marines. I was operating with 1/26 as I remember—more than forty-five years ago in the An Hoa area. We were scheduled to do a MedCap at a local village at the request of one of the South Vietnamese leaders. We went into the village, landing just short of the actual village itself. It was about two to three miles east of An Hoa and its airstrip. The MedCap is a means of helping South Vietnamese on what insurgency specialists call the "hearts and minds" aspect of our regimental operations. We were able to get several additional physicians other than just our battalion doctors and corpsmen to help us on this MedCap. The Vietnamese government, at whose request we were doing the MedCap, had done a better-than-average prescreening to do a form of triage, trying to, within their capacity and capabilities, single out the higher priority medical cases. I was satisfied that we had appropriate security for our docs doing their MedCap and that they were making good progress. I decided to take a helicopter (UH-Huey) back to Hill 55 and try to get some lunch. I had missed lunch already several times that week because I was en route to one of our battalions for command visits by me and members of my staff.

My helicopter took off and began gaining altitude over our MedCap village. The right door to our Huey was open, and I had my flight helmet on so that I could hear, using the guard channel, and talk directly to the pilot or copilot (if we had one). As a fixed-wing pilot usually flying in private-rental, general-aviation aircraft, I had been flying for about twenty-five years since leaving Quantico as a young second lieutenant in 1945. I estimated we were at about five hundred feet when I noticed an older Vietnamese gentleman, maybe around seventy-five years old, digging furiously just below the surface of a farmer's field as we were passing over it.

Suddenly he pulled out what appeared to be a rifle, wrapped in plastic. He spotted our chopper overhead, quickly removed the plastic wrapper from his weapon, shook it, and then aimed it at us. I was on the intercom with the pilots instantly and warned them that we had an older gentleman about to take some shots at us. I do not remember if our pilot started to jinx or quickly change direction before he fired. I warned everyone in the Huey to stand by for ground fire. At that moment, I saw a puff of smoke from his weapon, a French hunting rifle, and at the same time heard a "whang" as the round hit our aircraft.

I told the pilot that he might have hit something significant. We tried to see where he hit us. We couldn't, but all of us felt that he had hit the after portion of our chopper and were still looking for whatever damage we could find. I suggested to the pilot that we make a precautionary landing.

A precautionary landing is an immediate landing made to check something out, for example, where or if we had been hit. He agreed and suggested that we wait thirty seconds so we could land at An Hoa airstrip, in a protected area. I agreed so we sweated the thirty more seconds until landing at An Hoa. He wisely kept our altitude until we got to the protection of An Hoa airstrip below and then landed.

As we flew over the firing position, out of the corner of my eye, I spotted the old Vietnamese gentleman rewrapping and trying to bury his hunting rifle as quickly as possible. We landed without incident, and both the pilot and I ran around the tail of the aircraft and opened the clamshell tail rotor covers. The tail rotor shaft, as I remember, is about 1.5 inches in diameter of steel and about five-feet long, running from the main rotor base to the tail rotor housing. I noted that the bullet had made a through-and-through puncture hole right through the exact center of the tail rotor shaft. I knew that this was a chance hit and that the shooter had been very lucky to hit our tail rotor shaft. As a pilot, I suggested to our pilot that because it hit the shaft dead center, we had had a better chance for success in our precautionary landing. If it had been off center, considering the stresses that the tail rotor shaft takes in landing, it probably would have sheared. The pilot agreed.

This incident made me think that when you are sitting in a flying helicopter with no known damage, you feel somewhat invulnerable with your door gunner manning his weapon at all times when coming in or taking off from a landing.

One immediately wants revenge for the kind of damage that this old gentlemen wrought on our aircraft. Most of us flying in Vietnam therefore used to take the additional precaution of having a loaded, ready-to-fire door gun and gunner "at the ready." Had that MedCap helicopter belonged to me, that old gentlemen and his French hunting rifle would have been taken out instantly.

CHAPTER 26

Retiring from the Corps
1968-1970

The time had come for me to return to the United States after thirteen months in country. As a regimental commander, I made it to Hawaii to spend a day. I was, of course, eager to get home. FMF PAC pulled every regimental commander off returning aircraft to debrief them on lessons learned. We provided as much info as we could, and I have to believe it did fill in some of the FMF PAC staff on some of our activities. The next day, I was aboard a plane and happily returning to the States.

I reported in to Marine Corps schools, and Lt. Gen. Jeff Fields assigned me as exec for Col. Gene Haffey, who was CO of TBS. I enjoyed my one year as XO, but after TBS, I decided to practice law. This required taking the Virginia bar, which I did and passed. I retired in August 1970 with twenty-eight years of service and no regrets. My last year was at the Marine Corps Development Center to allow me to take the Virginia bar. It worked out well. Jo and each of my three boys, Craig, Boots, and Kit, were tremendously supportive of my retirement from the service and my entry as an attorney into what I found to be a very honorable profession.

Preparing for Retirement from the Corps

Having made the decision, as a family, to retire from the Marine Corps, we approached it as you would approach any major decision that was going to affect us all individually. We had our usual family discussions about what our new life was going to be like. We discussed where we would like to live in Seattle and what life working for a law firm would entail. We considered what adjustments we might have to make with Jo's family, who had lived in Seattle the entire twenty-eight years I was in the Marine Corps.

In 1963, I was graduating from law school while I was finishing up my tour of duty in Washington, D.C. We had our new house in Alexandria and all our friends and peers were being reassigned, most of them about the same rank (lieutenant colonel) and age as me, about forty. I knew from the experience of our friends the stresses I would encounter as a student in the Senior School. In a way, we anticipated the peer pressures that would be on me, competing with my friends of many years and many past duty stations. We put any fears aside, knowing I could only do the best that was possible. Having just completed the rigors of being a law student, I felt self-confident about my coming educational evaluation by the Marine Corps. I had done well in law school despite the unusual twelve-year gap between my first year of law school in 1949-1950 at the University of Washington and the resumption of my legal education in 1961 at George Washington University. I met those challenges and had been selected as an editor of the George Washington Law Review. I ended up fifth in my class and had been selected for the Order of the Coif, which meant that I had been tested in my legal education and had finished in the top one to two percent of graduating law students.

We knew it was going to be a risk, waiting six years from graduation from law school in 1963 to be sitting for a state or federal bar exam six years later in 1970. I was going to take two bar review courses, one right after the other. This took two nights a week, and the classes were held only in Washington, D.C. As usual, when we had undertaken special projects in the past, the entire family had kept on schedule with meals, and I got to my special classes on time. The boys kept the noise level down so I could study in the basement. I can assure you that there was great celebration when we found out that I had passed the Virginia bar. Then, I took the Washington State bar and passed it seven months later.

My Last Hurrah at the Marine Corps Development Center Urgent Testing of Marine Aviation's SPIE Rig (Special Patrol Insertion and Extraction)

SOMETIMES WHEN YOU ARE ASKED as a senior officer to help out on a problem, and you know within your heart that you can make a difference, you take that step. I found myself in such a situation when I was in charge of ground combat development at the Marine Corps Development Center. This was just two months before my retirement, which had actually been scheduled the previous year. At Quantico, I received a call from an agitated aviator general at HQMC. He knew that I was a qualified test parachutist and had done quite a bit of experimental work at what used to be the Naval Parachute Test Center, now designated as Naval Aviation Aero Recovery Facility. For simplicity, I shall refer to them simply as Naval Parachute Facility, El Centro.

Headquarters Marine Corps had received an urgent request requiring immediate response to the Marine air wings in Vietnam. The air wing's CH-46 helicopters had to make emergency extractions of Marine recon teams operating behind enemy lines in high- canopy jungle. The air wing was very concerned about continued use of an in-country extraction system being used by their helicopters to extract these recon personnel on an emergency basis. It is difficult to explain what was going through my mind when this problem arose. Here I was the most senior (non-general) officer responsible for the equipment and weapons that were to be examined, designated as necessary, and then tested before our Corps acquired the new gear for our Marines in the field. This was the mission of ground combat. That is why my title in the table of organization (T/O) is listed as chief of ground combat. Since I was the one who came up with many of the ideas of emplacement of highly trained recon Marines deep behind enemy lines, I felt a responsibility to ensure that once we inserted our teams behind enemy lines, we would be able to get them out by extraction. I kept thinking "You helped get them in there, now, make sure that you can recover them and get them out."

Our Marine pilots were expressing doubts regarding the continued usage of this jury-rigged, in-country, manufactured extraction system that they were being forced to use to pull surrounded recon Marine teams out from deep jungle. The air wing needed immediate evaluation of their jury-rigged system to ensure its flight safety. Headquarters Marine Corps had called El Centro and was given a laid-back reply that we could do this later. It was Friday, and we had a lot to do if we were going to resolve the air wing's safety problem.

I called El Centro immediately and asked for parachute engineer Howard Fish, whom I had worked with in the past when we were first developing parachuting operationally from carrier-based jet aircraft. He responded instantly and told me to come out and they would, as a matter of highest priority, do the testing they felt necessary to get the in-country, jury-rigged extraction devices fully certified. I convinced Fish of the life and death situation that we both faced. He told me to come out and unless we ran into major problems, we would have our rigs fully checked out and certified by the next week. I called my aviator general at HQMC, and he helped facilitate high priority air delivery of twelve rigs made to replicate the Vietnam-designed extraction rigs. Their highly qualified parachute engineers went over them literally stitch by stitch, inch by inch. The strength or lift-carrying capacity of a section of aircraft parachute webbing is determined by the number and spacing of the nylon parachute thread stitches. I grabbed one of my parachutists in the development center, and we flew that Sunday to El Centro with Capt. Norm Hisler.

In the meantime, I had my agitated Marine aviator general lay on two CH-46 helicopters from MCAS El Toro to be at El Centro the next week. The mission would include a ten- to twelve-Marine recon team in the jungle, surrounded with wounded and KIAs, and they had to be extracted. Our extraction rig was two pieces of two-inch nylon parachute webbing sewn back to back, at the bottom of the 120 feet of webbing were metal D-rings. The surrounded Marines could hook into the net and be extracted from the enemy surrounding them. The parachute riggers worked over the weekend on their own El Centro designs as Capt. Hisler and I were flying out to El Centro. Basically, their rigs were the same as ours. The El Centro design included an integrated parachute harness to be worn by all recon Marines when they were on the ground. All recon Marines carry carabiners that are identical to those that we carry when mountain climbing or rappelling using climbing rope. The carabiners can be used to hook into the D-rings, exactly as found on every U.S. military parachute. It was a simple solution, but it worked. The surrounded team has only to hook up with carabiners the bodies of any wounded or KIAs, so no one is ever left behind.

On Monday and Tuesday of the week, El Centro parachute engineers completed a detailed examination of both the in-country version and the NPU design. They had already lifted articulated same-weight 270-pound dummies to ensure lift safety. Our ever-present Navy flight surgeons were concerned about the psychological effects and feelings of the recon Marines who would be hanging 120 feet below the bottom of the CH-46 Boeing Vertol helicopters at two thousand to three thousand feet in the air. I had concluded that whoever was the bottom team member, at the base of the twelve D-rings, was going to have a strong role in the landings of the twelve team members coming down on top of the bottom person. I placed myself in that position so that I could articulate to our flight surgeon any problems that we encountered. They wired a standard Navy flight helmet with an oxygen mask so that I could record any of my observations. This was wired to a frequency so that I could talk to the pilot or crew as well. All transmissions were recorded for later analysis. Our flight surgeon had me wired with sensors, just like astronauts, to monitor my heart rate, respiration,

First live validation tests on SPIE (Special Patrol Insertion and Extraction) Rig, Naval Parachute Unit, El Centro, California, 1970.

body temps, and vital signs during all of our flight tests.

My recorded voice description of the hookup and then the lift off was followed by my sensations in flying fifteen hundred feet above the desert and then the descent. The helicopter achieved a "high hover" at a hundred twenty feet above the ground, slowly descending until the first of the twelve bodies arrived on the ground, trying to get out of the way as the next two landed, and so on. As you land, all of your higher-up-the-line teammates above you are also descending. I felt it was like a scrum from soccer or football. All reports from the debriefings, following the actual emergency extractions, were very positive with expressions of euphoria by each of the team members. As a qualified experimental parachutist, I rigged a small chestpack, which was similar to a standard T-7 reserve parachute, and I had the rigger fabricate a bungeed-nylon safety cover so that the rip cord on the reserve parachute could not be inadvertently activated. When the helicopter was making turns in flight, at fifteen hundred feet over the desert, we found that the hundred-twenty-foot extraction rig would trail out at a forty-five degree angle to the vertical. It was much like being towed on a sled on a frozen lake. The rig tried to stay vertical below the bottom of the towing helicopter, which itself was rotated from the vertical by doing a standard aviation turn.

The flight surgeon expected the data from my body signs and voice that had been recorded to change as we did maneuvers, descended, or climbed. We were doing about sixty to seventy knots during most of these maneuvers, the equivalent of about eighty-five miles per hour. He noted a modest increase in both respiration and blood pressure. I was unaware of these changes to my body. Our tests were completed in good order. The SPIE rigs, both versions, the in-country one made by the air wing riggers in Vietnam and the El Centro version, were approved for continued use.

This approval was immediately sent to the Marine air wing in Vietnam. The routine deep-insert patrols from the force recon companies had twenty-four to thirty inserts going each day, only a very few of which had to use the extraction rig. The vast majority of team retrievals were facilitated by a quick landing and loading, then liftoff by the recovery helicopter. Most inserts and recoveries were executed by Huey helicopters, not gunships. After all of the evaluations were completed, I briefed my general, CG of the Marine Corps Development Center at Quantico, Maj. Gen. Al Armstrong, who just happened to be an aviator. His comment to me, "You made a lot of friends today among Marine pilots and the recon guys they carry. Well done."

My last year was spent at the development center to enable me to take the Virginia bar exam. It worked out well. Jo and I had been married more than twenty-two years, and Craig, Boots, and Kit were tremendously supportive of my retirement from the service and entry into law. I found being an attorney to be an honorable profession, following in the footsteps of my deceased father and grandfather, who had both been lawyers, and I felt them looking over my shoulder. Our eldest son, Craig, became a lawyer and served twenty-one years of active duty as a Marine Corps judge advocate, retiring as a lieutenant colonel. He now serves as an assistant attorney general of the United States in the Justice Department in Washington, D.C.

Leaving the Corps and Taking My Family Overseas

I RECEIVED A MODEST AMOUNT of money for unused leave from the Marine Corps when I retired. I believe it was about $1,200. Then we decided that while we were on the east coast, it would be less expensive to take the entire family to Europe for three weeks now rather than later when we retired in Seattle. We got a special rate for the entire family. We flew out of New York, which was more affordable than Washington, D.C. We rented a midsize Opel station wagon in Frankfurt, Germany. The entire family was involved in the trip planning. We drove from Frankfurt through France, then to Switzerland, and on to Italy and Rome and Naples. We went up the

Rhone Valle, from Marseilles to Paris, east through Holland and Belgium, and then back to Frankfurt for the return flight to New York. Looking back on it, this was one of our most memorable family trips. While we were away, we left our two small wirehaired terriers with one of my former TBS Marine officers, Capt. Bob LeRoy, in his Manhattan apartment.

One humorous aspect of driving the German car was that as we were on the autobahn in Germany or on autoroute in France or autostrade in Italy, other German cars with German license plates would flash their headlights and honk as we passed them, obviously thinking we were German. Jo and I would always alert the three boys and it became a game. We would say, "Look German," and the boys would appropriately sit up and somehow look studious or intense. My apologies to our German friends. At the time, the summer of 1970, it brought a bit of humor to those long autobahn drives. It was a tiring trip, but everyone, particularly our boys, got a lot out of it. It had so impressed our oldest son, Craig, who was fifteen at the time, that he vowed that he was going to get a job, save his money, and come back the following summer by himself. He would fly into Frankfurt, and then hitchhike or ride the trains cheaply with a Eurorail pass.

He was able to get a job flipping hamburgers at Jack in the Box. He saved his money, paid his own fare, bought a Eurorail pass at a cheaper rate by buying it ahead of time in the United States. We alerted a retired Marine friend, Lt. Col. Dave "M.A." Girard, who was working in Germany and living with his wife. Craig would visit them in Germany to get his laundry done and eat a square meal. He and the college girls he was escorting would stay overnight in youth hostels wherever they were. They managed to get by on two meals a day, breakfast and dinner. They bought other food at farmer's markets and from street vendors to keep their costs down.

To assure his mother that he would be safe, I gave Craig a list of senior Marine master sergeants from the Marine Embassy guards for every country in Europe. If he got into any trouble or had a problem, he could contact one of them. He did not need to contact them during his three-month-long trip, but we felt better knowing that he had their names, just in case. Craig managed to make friends with young American college girls who would seize on Craig to be their traveling companion. These American college girls realized that if they had a rather large, six-foot-three-inch American male with them, they would not be pinched or hit on by the local Italian, French, or German men. Looking back, I believe Craig came home a fairly sophisticated twenty-five-year-old, despite being only sixteen. After about two weeks on the road, he stashed his backpack in Switzerland and only carried a small sleeping bag, hung on a thin rope, and carried anything else in the pockets of one of my old

Marine field jackets. It apparently worked fine as a travel system; he traveled from Bodo, Norway, to Greece and Crete, where he slept in farmers' fields. We were proud of his independence and pleased that he took advantage of getting an early start on his university work by taking a number of university-level courses while he was in high school. Jo about had apoplexy when I gave him permission to go to Europe on his own at sixteen. He went on to finish law school and have a successful twenty-one-year career in the Marines, a lieutenant colonel when he retired.

Pleasant Farewell from the French Foreign Legion

WE WERE DRIVING UP the southern coastline of France, as we approached Marseilles, which was our first port of call at the start of our Mediterranean cruise. Marseilles lies at the southern entrance to the Rhone Valley en route to Paris and Frankfurt for our return flight. Just east of Marseilles (about twelve kilometers) is a small French village called Aubagne. This is where the administrative headquarters of the worldwide French Foreign Legion is located. In the two months that the Second Battalion, Parachutist, French Foreign Legion was attached for operational training to my Sixth Fleet landing force, I had never been to Aubagne but had always operated with their headquarters on the island of Corsica at Fort Bonifacio. Basically, the Second Battalion of parachutists had been part of my command for a two-month period.

I sensed that the Legion did not, as a usual matter, mind having a German station wagon with German plates on it pulling up to their sentry building. The senior sergeant came to my driver door. I greeted him in French, identified myself as a recently retired colonel of the United States Marines. I advised him that the Second Battalion had been under my command on Corsica and I had brought my family back to France to visit the Legion Musée at Aubagne. This caused a reaction that I had not expected. He immediately called the officer of the day to alert him. He then broke out the twelve to fifteen legionnaires and asked if I would honor them by inspecting his guard. I took this as an honor and did the most formal type of inspection that I had learned with the Legion on Corsica. I complimented the sergeant and the captain duty officer on "the fine appearance" of his legionnaires. The officer of the day had called for the curator of the Musée to take "the Col. and his family for an official tour of the French Foreign Legion Museum." An older (about forty to forty-five years) French Foreign Legion captain approached us and introduced himself. His uniform and demeanor were indeed memorable. He was wearing the white *kepi* (uniform hat) with a polished black bill; his uniform was impeccable and well decorated with the highest of French medals, among them was the *Croix de Guerre*. He was wearing a black eye patch on one eye, and his face displayed an evident saber scar. He was using a cane, his left wrist had been shot off, and he had a metal and wood prosthetic wrist and hand. Had we put in a request to central casting for a highly decorated officer of the French Foreign Legion, we could have done no better.

He spent two hours guiding us through the museum in a thorough but informational visit. In an atmosphere that was almost religious in nature, he took us to an obviously revered section with low lighting, just a single spotlight suspended from high in the ceiling. Displayed on a gorgeous red pillow was the carved wooden arm of the Legion's greatest hero, Capt. D'Anjou, whose wooden arm had been returned by the Mexican ambassador, recovered after the sixty-eight legionnaires' stunning defeat at Camerone in central Mexico in the War with Maximilian April 30, 1863. He then turned to our three boys and asked very formally: "Would the gentlemen and the lady join us for a cocktail in our officer's mess?" We all eagerly accepted his invitation. Our boys (I am sure) expected to be given a cocktail of sorts. They each got a Coke. Jo and I enjoyed a light French wine.

Knowing the legionnaires great pride in their hero Capt. D'Anjou and his troop of sixty-eight legionnaires, I have worn a medallion featuring Capt. D'Anjou around my neck since it was given to me by the Second Parachute Battalion. It was with me my entire tour in Vietnam. Our guide was obviously very touched to learn later that a colonel of the U.S. Marine Corps was wearing this French medallion, and that I had worn it at the battle of Khe Sanh and ever since. We expressed our appreciation and then departed.

CHAPTER 27

Practice of Law
1970-2010

We drove to Seattle where I got a great position with an old, distinguished law firm and enjoyed the next thirty years living on Mercer Island, a bedroom community close to Seattle. After more than four straight years of trial work as a litigation attorney, I was a bit tired of a jury trial every month. I received a call from the founding dean of a relatively new law school, at an old and well-loved university, the University of Puget Sound. I accepted the positions of associate dean and associate professor. As associate dean, I was asked to run the law school, which I did. I also was able to teach as the associate professor. It was a good fit, and I did not miss the Marine Corps as much as some of my peers had predicted. Jo and I missed our good friends who were always the best of lasting friendships.

Following a year managing a large- to medium-sized old and prestigious firm of Lane, Powell, Moss & Miller with thirty-five attorneys, and, having passed the Washington bar on my first try, I had the opportunity to join a smaller firm, Reed, McClure, Moceri and Thonn, as a litigator. I quickly picked up the pace in this firm known for its aggressive insurance defense practice.

One of the senior partners, Hugh McClure, had been a classmate of mine when I first went to law school at the University of Washington in 1949-1950. After having a more-experienced attorney from my new firm sit through two of my jury trials,

Bruce F. Meyer, Attorney at Law.

I was cut loose and began an intense four years of trial practice doing nothing but litigation, mostly in jury trials. As all litigation attorneys do, I was started out on modest cases, slips-and-falls, property damage, and then automobile cases with increasingly complex medical damages and medical issues. I then received police defense cases because our firm had a contract with the insurance carrier that insured most of the Northwest police departments. The word somehow got out that I had done some police work and had undergone a short FBI course while working as National Park ranger, before coming back on active duty for the Korean War. I believe that this experience made the police more comfortable with me when I was defending them.

OLD HABITS DIE HARD. I have always kept a short haircut, and I always made a special effort to look what Marines called "squared away." Shoes were always polished to a fare-thee-well. I usually wore a white shirt and a "regimental" striped tie, and most of the time a dark suit. My defense cases of police departments and errant officers ran the gamut from high-speed chases, where someone was injured or killed, frequently the case when miscreants were fleeing; excessive force; and mistaken arrest of persons that were in insulin shock for driving under the influence.

It seemed that I was trying a number of insulin shock cases. When a police department is sued, usually the police chief is joined as a defendant by private attorneys who would like to sue police departments. Hence, I was soon on a first name basis with Tacoma's chief of police, Lyle Smith. He was very professional, and probably one of the best chiefs that I have defended. He was a graduate of the long police course at Quantico that lasted six months. When I was commanding officer at the Basic School, our location at Quantico was next to the FBI Academy. Naturally, I got to know a number of directors and instructors at the FBI Academy. I would be invited to fire on their rifle and pistol ranges and fire their specialized weapons. It was a good relationship.[1]

Over a one-year period, I defended the Tacoma police in a number of cases of excessive force where the officers used their billy clubs to gain control of someone they thought was a DUI (drunk driver). After about seven or eight of these excessive force cases, I had gotten to know the difference between the symptoms of a DUI arrestee and someone who was a diabetic and was in insulin shock. Many of the symptoms are almost identical, so I could understand why the police would frequently misread the subject being arrested as being drunk: slurred speech, blurry eyes, instability in walking, exuding a distinctive smell, and other aberrant behaviors. I discussed the symptoms and the mistaken diagnoses with our county medical examiner (CME). He agreed that he and I could put together a short course on the different symptoms of DUI versus diabetic shock to reduce the number of mistaken diagnosis by arresting officers. I went to the chief of Tacoma police and asked to be able to give a thirty-minute course with all officers doing patrol duty. (Most of these misdiagnoses took place during evening hours.)

We divided all the patrol officers into two sessions, and I taught them and the CME, two nights in a row. Looking back, I felt that what I was doing to educate these police patrol officers was preventative law, where something is done to reduce or eliminate a possible violation of a citizen's rights. I suggested to the chief that all patrol cars start carrying some hard candy and a small bottle of orange juice because both are effective in bringing someone out of diabetic insulin shock. They did, and with their new awareness of such things as rigidity against being pulled from their autos, the number of cases of misreading insulin shock as DUIs dropped dramatically. The department was happy, our insurance company was happy, and the only people who did not like what I had done were the plaintiff's attorneys who brought the excessive force cases.

...

---

1 On one occasion, our CG had a conflict and could not be at the FBI Academy to escort the Director, J. Edgar Hoover, who was visiting Quantico, to lay a cornerstone for a new FBI Academy building. I was asked to fill in for my missing general to escort Mr. Hoover. My friends, who were agents, all warned me that Mr. Hoover detested sweaty palms. Because we were aware of this, when we had to shake hands, you could see people in the line more or less rubbing their hands on their pants so they were not sweaty.

Teaching from Real-World Experiences

Many years later, when I was teaching first-year law students torts, the handling of personal injury cases and accidents and damages, I would occasionally give the police defense example. Some of my fellow law professors felt this was below what I should be teaching. My dean, Dean Joseph Sinclitico, was pleased because I was bringing some practical, useful knowledge into the law classroom. He said that in his experience in starting three new law schools, that many law professors tried to be more esoteric and teach on some higher plane. When teaching law, I always tried to bring some of the practical lessons learned from trials in an actual courtroom. Years later, while practicing law in Seattle, young attorneys who had been former law students of mine would stop me in the elevator and thank me for something that I had taught them.

I remember one case where, using the Socratic method, I brought a training aid to my law school class. We were discussing the flamboyant and nationally well-known San Francisco attorney, Melvin Belli, and his case of a young woman running to catch a cable car, who slipped and fell under the wheels and her leg was amputated. Belli had a plaster cast made of the missing leg, to its exact size and measurement. He then took it to his butcher shop and had the plaster leg wrapped in butcher paper and then he placed it on counsel table, right in front of where the jury could continually see it. The attorney for the defense should have immediately had the fake amputated leg removed as an item that exacerbated the jury. In order to make the point of the fact that defense counsel should have objected, which he did not do in the Belli case, I decided to bring a training aid. I drove to a medical prosthetics shop located on hospital hill, or Pill Hill, in Seattle. I asked the attendant if his store ever had a spare prosthetic leg. The salesperson looked at me as if I was bereft of sense. He said, "Yes, as a matter of fact I do have one. We made it for an old gentlemen, and before he could pick it up, he died." I asked if there was any use for the prosthetic leg. He asked why I wanted it. When I told him that I was a law professor and wished to use it on a case that we were discussing, he advised that they really had no further use for it. I could have it if I wished. I offered to pay him, and he said that the insurance company had already paid for it, and a prosthetic leg cannot be reused, once it is made. "It only would fit the person for whom it was made. Here, take it." I did, and I took it to my butcher shop, where I paid the butcher to "make this look like a piece of meat as much as you can."

On the day of the class on the Belli amputee case, I placed my "leg" on what would be the counsel table. Four women in the front row were obviously upset by my actions. They were furious and were going to go to our dean and file a complaint against me "for insulting and embarrassing the class." Fortunately, I had anticipated the possibility of such a reaction amongst the female law students. I explained what I was doing and why to the dean. He was enthusiastic and was quite prepared to face the wrath of the offended female law students. The women raced to his office and began berating me for my insensitivity. The dean stopped their rant and told them that they had been privy to one of the best practical, real-world teaching examples that he was aware of in any law school. He told the women, now regretting their reaction, they had been given an excellent lesson—one that they never would forget. They respected Dean Joseph Sinclitico, a Harvard University honors graduate. I assure you that my use of the prosthetic leg obviously became a critical memory of when to object and when not to sit on your hands and see their defense case go down the tube. I have been stopped by former students a half dozen times and thanked for the practicality of my teaching law, the leg being just one example.

I ENJOYED CLASSROOM TEACHING, but the drain of continuous administrative work began to take its toll.

My son Craig completed law school and worked for a year as a trial assistant to a very distinguished attorney in Seattle. He took and passed the Washington bar and then opted to enter the Marine Corps as an attorney in the Judge Advocate Gen. (JAG) corps. He completed a distinguished Marine Corps career and now is one of the senior assistant attorney generals in the Justice Department as head of their environmental law division in Washington, D.C. Our middle son, Bruce Jr. ("Boots"), had three years at the University of Washington and left of his own volition to do commercial fishing in Alaska and construction. Our youngest son, Christopher, concentrated on commercial banking. At the time of his death, he was vice president of the Republic Bank home office in Dallas, Texas.

During my sixth year as associate dean and as an associate professor, there was typical law school faculty pressure urging me to get an LLM (masters in law). Usually a sabbatical in teaching is given in the seventh year. I was going to lose my Vietnam GI Bill unless I could go one year early (my sixth year). Meeting almost weekly with the University of Puget Sound President Phil Phibbs, I approached him and requested permission to take my sabbatical one year early to avoid the loss of my Vietnam GI Bill. He asked me what I wanted to do in academe. I told him that I wanted to become better educated in medicine, so that I could better teach a law school course in law and medicine. When he asked where I hoped to go, I answered that I had chosen pairs of top-tier schools that both excelled in law and medicine. He agreed and urged me to continue my learning. I applied and was accepted at Stanford, the University of Michigan, and the University of Virginia. Harvard had not made its decision, although their masters course took one hundred students. Yale University only took twelve Americans in their masters' program along with twelve foreign students. When Yale admitted me as a fellow, I accepted.

My courses were split between Yale Medical School and Yale Law School. The deans of the law and medical schools got together and created a good balance of classes, which meant that I had to commute across the city of New Haven to the medical school in West Haven. I joined seven medical students, all in their third year. It was an intense year, and I learned much. In my seminar, "Medicine of the Chronically Ill," my med classmates had renal patients, diabetic patients, orthopedic patients, and others. I was assigned a schizophrenic patient. We met weekly and then the students had seminars together with each of us making reports to our fellow seminar medical students. I had to presume that they assigned me a schizophrenic and his psychiatrist because they felt that a retired Marine officer with seven years as a trial lawyer could relate somehow to my schizophrenic patient.

Agent Orange

IN A YALE MEDICAL SCHOOL COURSE on toxic substances,"they asked me what toxic substances I wished to research. Without hesitation I responded "dioxin." The professor, whom I had gotten to know, asked me why. I responded that in Vietnam, as a regimental commander, I was one of the largest users of dioxin, also called Agent Orange, a very toxic defoliant. Research went well, and I managed to get some information from the CIA. I wrote the article, and my professor suggested sending it to the *Boston College Environmental Law Review*.

Christmas at Yale had all of our classmates going home to Wisconsin, Florida, and several other states. Having just indexed a medical book at Yale for which I was paid $600, Jo and I decided to fly "space available" (you occupy any empty seat on military aircraft going everywhere in the world) to Europe. We flew into Frankfurt and took the train down to the beaches of Spain. Upon our return to Yale, our telephone was ringing off the hook. *Boston College Environmental Law Review* was asking, in essence, "What the hell did you write?" I innocently asked why they were asking. They said that, once the law review containing my article was published, they had received an order for five hundred copies of my issue. They told me that never before in the history of Boston College had they ever received such a request. It seemed that my article, "Agent of Orange," chronicling the history and use of dioxin-based defoliant, particularly in Vietnam, was "the article of interest" for the scientific community. I received calls from scientists and physicians from all over the world, including Sweden and Australia, to name a few. I was called to report to the Queen's Royal Commission on Agent Orange. This was Britain's study of the effects of Agent Orange on their empire's support of our troops in Vietnam. I testified before the ongoing Agent Orange litigation in the Long Island Federal District Court.

Returning to Practice

MY MEDICAL PROFESSORS AT YALE were pleased, and the rest of the year went well. Upon re-entry into the Seattle bar, practicing in a small two-attorney firm, I began to do a fairly lucrative arbitration and mediation practice, as well as defense for Seattle Metro (the Seattle transit system). I was elected chair of the Washington State Bar Committee on Alternate Dispute Resolution (ADR), where I was editor-in-chief. The state bar published my attorney deskbook, *Alternate Dispute Resolution Deskbook,* titled "Arbitration and Mediation in Washington." It was published in three editions over the next three years. My chapter authors and I gave continuing legal education (CLE) presentations throughout the state, accompanied by distribution of the deskbook.

In Retirement

IN 2008, AFTER PRACTICING LAW for forty years, I decided to retire and do some writing. I have had two military history books published: *Fortune Favors the Brave* (155,000 copies) and *Swift, Silent and Deadly* (5,000 copies) by Naval Institute Press and St. Martin's Press, respectively. I was later approached by my Sgt. Maj. Neal King, and together we agreed to design and build a monument dedicated to Marines, corpsmen, and families of the force recon companies and MARSOC. We raised more than $18,000 in donations and had it built and installed at the National Museum of the Marine Corps at Quantico.

All bills were paid. We have paid for future maintenance as we and our monument age. It was dedicated on the Marine Corps birthday in 2010, located just two feet from the Chesty Puller paved walkway. A paved walkway permits wheelchairs complete access to circle our monument. It is located in Semper Fi Park, about two hundred yards from the museum at Quantico, and one block down the hill from the chapel. We have traveled to most all places where I served as well as to many new places which now have become pleasant memories.

• • •

Col. Bruce Meyers at the dedication of the monument honoring force recon and MARSOC Marines, corpsmen, and their families, November 10, 2012, on the anniversary of the unit's founding. The monument is at the Marine Corps Museum, Quantico, Virginia.

CHAPTER 28

Passing the Torch

With the reality of life, we all recognize that we will eventually die. That is truth, and we naturally do not look forward to dying, yet each of us is aware that we will lose friends and loved ones. When I started to write down what I hoped to share with my two sons, thoughts came up about deaths and how they are a part of life. We celebrate a person's life, and when they are gone, we take that moment to reflect on how they influenced us.

I am not enthused about funerals. For a time we mourn the loss, yet I also think about what the person did in their life. Hence, I manage to take funerals in stride. They are just another part of life. Over thousands of years, we have developed our celebration of a person's life when they die. In the military, we have developed passage that permits recognition of our honorable profession.

I have been asked close to a hundred times to present the flag, the symbol of the deceased service to our corps and country. We all learn the ritual of holding the colors with our hands above and below. For most military funerals, I always try to dress in blues, with full (large) medals. We walk slowly and solemnly and approach the next of kin with grace. I usually kneel on one knee, and place the colors in the hands of the recipient, and utter the reverent words "On behalf of a grateful nation." I then stand, take one step backward, and render a ceremonial hand salute, and then slowly lower my salute and ease away. During this part of the ceremony, the playing of "Taps" may occur. Whenever "Taps" is played, one comes to attention and renders a hand salute, with a ceremonial (slow) lowering and resumption of attention. Sometimes Taps may be followed by a playing of a military song that is fitting for the ceremony: the "Marine Corps Hymn," the "Navy Hymn," or "Amazing Grace." My mother was of Scottish ancestry, so for any funerals that I help out on, I coordinate with the funeral director, the chaplain, the priest, the reverend, or the family for possible use of a bagpiper. I always ensure that the piper and the priest are coordinated on sequence of such events.

Induction into University of Washington NROTC Wall of Fame

THE LAST MILITARY ACTIVITY involving me took place just as the writing of this book was completed. It is emblematic of those of us who were fortunate to receive our officer training at the first NROTC unit ever established in the United States. This was the first of six such units established in 1926 at the University of Washington Naval ROTC and five other universities: University of California at Berkley, Northwestern University, Georgia Tech, Harvard, and Yale. Most of us were midshipmen who went through University of Washington and became Navy and Marine officers. We have good memories of the training that we received. It was a surprise that recognition came to some of us who served as a result of our training at the UW NROTC unit.

The UW NROTC recently notified Rear Adm. Herb Bridge[1] and me, advising us of our induction into the UW NROTC Wall of Fame, which occurred September 7, 2013, at Clark Hall at the University of Washington. Of the first five Naval service graduates who were inducted, Herb and I were the only ones still alive for the induction ceremony. Deceased inductees included Col. Greg "Pappy" Boyington, USMC, MOH[2] Guadalcanal, twenty-eight kills; Brig. Gen. Robert Gayler, USMC, MOH Guadalcanal, fourteen kills; and Rear Adm. Bob Copeland, Navy Cross, CO, DE *Samuel B. Roberts* sunk in Battle of Leyte Gulf when the ship attacked the entire Japanese fleet, saving the landing force in the Leyte invasion.

We had the honor of escorting a longtime friend, Seaman Jack Yuson, the last living survivor of the sinking of the *Samuel B. Roberts* and who survived after spending fifty hours with the sharks off Leyte Gulf.

1 Herb Bridge was a high school friend who ran track with the author. Later they were classmates at the University of Washington and members of the U\university's Naval ROTC unit. See the last paragraph, Chapter 3.
2 Medal of Honor.

Speakers at the induction ceremony were Admiral Bridge, who was recalled to active duty for the Vietnam War, in charge of all shipping, military, and civilian cargo destined for Vietnam; Capt. Dave Mellin, professor of naval science and tactics, who was the spearhead for this very worthy project to provide recognition for our NROTC heroes and achievers; and me, the USMC regimental commander of the Twenty-Sixth Marines and Khe Sanh in longest battle of the Vietnam War.

Afterword

After retirement from the Marine Corps, I continued to travel to the Far East. I have been back to Korea twice and Japan a number of times, and I've made four trips to Vietnam.

My friend Col. Warren Wiedhahn formed a small group of former Marines to run tours back to battlefields. They run tours to the Pacific battlefields of WW II — Iwo, Okinawa, Australia, etc. On their later war tours, Warren asked me to lead some four tours, which I have done, back to the battlefields in I Corps Khe Sanh.

I started out more than fifteen years ago and led my first return to Khe Sanh. We usually start in Hanoi and get a briefing from the KIA/MIA[3] recovery team stationed in Hanoi. We spend half a day at the Hanoi Hilton Prison where Senator John McCain and others were held after their shoot-downs. We fly down to the I Corps area and go out to the various battlefields. We always spend about half a day revisiting Khe Sanh. We always place an assembly of flowers, and we say a few words of remembrance and then go back to our air,conditioned buses and head back down to the coast for Red Beach and Da Nang area.

My first trip back included retired Commandant Carl Mundy and his two Marine officer sons. Carl was great and made some remarks at our airstrip at Khe Sanh. Everyone has the chance to walk the battlefield to find "their place." Carl had served in my artillery battalion (1/13) during my time as commander near the end of the siege. He was a great addition and made our return a memorable event.

---

3   KIA/MIA: Killed in Action, Missing in Action.

The author and (right) Gen. Carl Mundy, Marine Corps Commandant .

The Healing Began

I NOTICED A VERY IMPORTANT PHENOMENON that occurred on that first trip on return. Whenever we got to a spot in walking the battlefield where someone in the group had been wounded or lost someone close, without exception they would each pretty much go through the same reaction—they began to cry, drop to the ground, and beat their hands on the ground. I have been twice diagnosed with post traumatic stress disorder (PTSD). When I got back from that first revisit to Khe Sanh, I asked both of my doctors what I could do to help these Marines and corpsmen from our Khe Sanh combat experience. Both said "Do what you are already doing. Take them back to the place they were wounded or lost someone close."

As a result, I then asked Military Historical Tours to find out from each of the returnees where their "special place" was located, and I would take a GPS locator with me, and we could usually find the location. The returning Marine would drop and beat the ground. Without any guidance, the rest of us would gather around the returnee, hug him, and as peers, having been through the same stresses, give him reassurance and make personal contact. All reacted in the same way and began to be able to talk about their experience. It was always astounding that most reacted in the same way.

I began to get phone calls from psychiatrists asking, "What the hell did you do for my patient?" I then would tell them the positive experience that each of us had in making the trip back to Vietnam. Their shrinks were impressed that this "return to Khe Sanh" had made a great change in their lives. They no longer suffered from flashbacks, and we suggested that they no longer view war movies. I reported these contacts with our returnees and their families. They were pleased that they had this experience. It was a side effect that none of us had anticipated. Looking back, I was glad to have participated with them in this "lifting the bad memories from their backs."

ON EACH OF THE FOUR "RETURN TO KHE SANH" TRIPS that I was asked to lead, I usually arranged for an informal service and placement of flowers at the site. On that first trip, now some fifteen years ago, retired Gen. Carl Mundy, who had been a young major in my artillery battalion when I was commanding the Twenty-Sixth Marines at Khe Sanh, recited the Marine Corps verse of the U.S. Navy. We were impressed and pleased by his reading:

Eternal Father, grant we pray,
To all Marines, both night and day,
The courage, honor, strength and skill our land to serve, Thy law fulfill .

* * *

Final Thoughts

I MISS JO, my wife of sixty-four years. I now have two of our sons and my great corgie, Amy, to share life with. I waited and then remarried in 2011. I also miss my second wife, Jean Kilby, who suffered an acute stroke shortly after we were married and is now hospitalized in Arizona. I thank God for my health and that I can still ambulate with relative ease. I am vertical and feel that I still enjoy cognizance. I yet remember the curve of a fine thigh, the look of a beautiful breast. I share a frozen Beefeaters with old friends. Life continues as best we can. We try to adjust to our life changes. One sage observation for my two adult sons, Craig and Boots: "Don't quit your day job if you write books."

After sixty-four years of marriage to Jo, I have found in being around, and commanding, recon Marines and our tremendous corpsmen, our families and wives in particular, are a collective of great bravery, beauty, understanding, and particularly stoicism and patience when they wait and support our Marines and corpsmen wearing our dive bubbles and jump wings.

Finally, this book is dedicated to my superb recon divers and parachutists, operators who always performed above and beyond anyone's expectation and were unfailingly brave in crisis. Without them this book could never have been written.

Semper Fidelis and God bless.

Bruce Meyers

Bruce F. Meyers, Col. USMC, Ret.

Medals and Honors

Decorations

- Bronze Star Medal w/Combat "V"
- Joint Force Commendation Medal (first ever awarded)
- Korean PUC w/three stars
- Legion of Merit w/Combat "V" (Valor)
- Navy Letter of Commendation Medal w/Combat "V"
- Navy Marine Corps Medal
- The Purple Heart
- United Nations Service Medal
- Vietnamese Cross of Gallantry with Palm (2nd Award)

Service Medals

- American Campaign Medal
- Asiatic-Pacific Campaign Medal
- Combat Action Medal
- Korean Service Medal w/five stars
- National Defense Service Medal w/one star
- Organized Marine Corps Reserve Medal
- Presidential Unit Citation (3 awards)
- Vietnam Campaign Medal
- Vietnam Service Medal w/three stars
- WW II Victory Medal

Special Qualifications

- Navy-Marine Corps Parachutist Insignia (Gold)
- Navy Diver Insignia (Silver)

In Appreciation

I owe sincere thanks to several people who made publication of this book possible:

Jim Harris, retired independent book sales representative, who saw my memoirs worthy of publication and got the ball rolling, putting me together with several friends in the business; **Stephen Lay**, manager of Epicenter Press, acting as advisor; **Jennifer McCord**, Jennifer McCord Associates LLC, editorial and publishing consultant; **Sheryl Stebbins,** editorial consultant; **Jeanie James**, book and cover designer, owner and creative director of Shorebird Creative; and **Vaughn Sherman**, author, owner, and manager of Patos Island Press LLC, who pulled together all the fine work of these people and published *Reflections of a Grunt Marine.*

I'm proud of the resulting book, and touched by the friendships that came out of working with this fine team of professionals.

Index

K

L

M

N

T

U